DON'T TAKE IT PERSONALLY

REAL *LOVE* KNOCKS THE HELL OUT OF YOU

Allison Bramlett

Allison Bramlett
Don't Take It Personally

Published by: Allison Bramlett
Text Design by: Robyn Soucinek & Jeribai Tascoe
Cover Design by: Allison Bramlett

A CIP record for this book is available from the Library of Congress Cataloging-in-Publication Data

ISBN: 978-0-578-37680-6

FOREWORD

by Kimberly Jones
(aka Real Talk Kim)

Throughout the book, Don't Take It Personally, we are encountering the love of Jesus as Allison takes you on a journey of forgiveness!

We are understanding that forgiveness is a choice, not an emotion! If we are always ruled by our feelings, we will be like the hamster on the wheel moving continually but getting nowhere while de-testing our lives. God got off His throne and onto the cross to show us how to forgive in spite of the pain and malice involved.

God gave the ultimate sacrifice with you in mind. He knew that you would need him twenty-four hours a day to be restored, revived, and renewed.

You may find yourself at a place feeling stuck, but Allison helps you navigate as you see how she makes it through day by day while focusing forward!

Allison lets us know that it is empowering when we choose to walk in God's love. It not only empowers us, but it protects us. When this love is evident, our identity can be secure in Him.

This book will give you direction as you determine to walk in love and forgiveness while allowing Jesus to be your compass as you navigate life's challenges. I am so thankful to be called Allison's friend as we journey through this life together.

INTRODUCTION

I think it's safe to say that no one signs up for a relationship hoping to get hurt and feel miserable. We don't plan on hurting others or making them miserable either! Instead, we enter into relationships with positive expectations. We expect to enjoy a good measure of satisfaction and pleasure, and as we are for the other person, we desire to see them win and win big. Yet, despite all that initial positivity, almost everyone I know struggles in relationships. I'm not just talking about marital relationships but also in relationships with family members, friends, colleagues… you name it.

So what are we to do when people disappoint, offend, and hurt us? How do we get past our own mistakes? And, as Jesus-followers, how are we to react or respond to not only those "minor cuts" that happen between two people but also those major "deep-cut" inflictions as well?

I say we run to our Creator to find healing with our own issues.

And, when others hurt us, we don't take things personally. Easy, right? Not exactly, but keep reading!

Jesus modeled this mindset for us when He hung on the cross, dying for our sins. He cried out, "'Father, forgive them for they do not know what they are doing'" (Luke 23:34). Simply put, Jesus did not take things personally. He knew, and we must know, that there is more going on in someone's life than what we can see. Ephesians 6:12 makes this clear: "For our struggle is not against flesh and blood, but against the rulers, against the authorities, against the powers of this dark world and against the spiritual forces of evil in the heavenly realms." This verse brought great freedom for me as I was able to understand that the wrestling matches in my life were not against people but against principalities. Knowing this (and reminding myself often) has helped me to not judge or make assumptions about others. I can choose compassion. I can choose forgiveness. I can choose love. This doesn't let them off the hook, but it has helped me to not be hooked in with them!

So, if you are a part of any relationship (and it's a safe bet that you are), let me begin by saying that this book is for you. Do you choose or want to choose to love even when you don't feel like it? Do you sometimes feel as if your life is a magnet for problems and dysfunction within relationships? Do you acknowledge the craziness and messiness of your life but struggle to remember that God's love is deeper and wider than any problem? If so, I believe these chapters are for you. I wrote them to remind you that, even in the midst of hardship and heartbreak with others, there is no one and no relationship more important than the one you can have with Jesus. He will help you with your other relationships because He is that powerful and that loving. He has already won the battle, so we do well when we stay close to Him and remember who we are in Him.

I believe that you can experience intimacy with Jesus far above what you can imagine and, as a result, any pain you have endured can become a distant, vague memory. I know because that's my story. So, this is for those who have struggled and fought just as I have to live beyond the pain. I believe that following the steps and promises of Jesus, the man who is love, is the only way to have victory in the fight!

My prayer is that you will know that your purpose is greater than any pain you have felt or will feel or have inflicted upon others. Your purpose is greater than the people who have hurt you, your colorful past, or any pettiness and pride you've endured or dished out. A lifetime of perfect relationships is impossible because we are all human. We make mistakes, hurt others, and we get hurt, but that doesn't mean we have to give up on love.

There's no other relationship I've had to learn this more than in my marriage. When my husband Jeff and I got married, we pledged our love and said our vows to each other. We declared "I do" to our promises, but we were also saying, "I do want a happily ever after with you." Yet it wasn't enough for us to want it, we had to choose it. I had to choose it. What my 18-year-old self pledged to him that day while standing at the altar, wearing a pretty white gown, and holding a bouquet of white roses, was that no matter the circumstances—for better or for worse, in sickness and in health, 'til death do us part… "I do." I made a sincere covenant vow before God and witnesses, though I could not fully grasp how that vow would require of me this continual choice: to fight the good fight of faith and stay in love with my husband whether or not he was loving or faithful to me.

The truth is, however, many times over the years, this has meant choosing to live in a covenant full of pain, broken promises, frustrations, and disappointments. I've had to choose, for example, to obey God when He has told me to keep my wedding ring on. More than once I've wanted to take that sparkly symbol of love and throw it far from me, but the Lord told me that I was married to Him first and foremost and that I was to choose to remain married to Jeff. So the ring has stayed on my finger. (Let me just say right out of the shoot that I do realize there are times when God releases someone from their marriage. Biblical grounds for divorce do exist, but ending the covenant is not God's intent for marriage.)

Perhaps you, too, have chosen to not get a divorce and to not let the past dictate your future. Maybe your kids and grandkids have been the sole reason for keeping your marriage together, or maybe there are enough glimpses of joy and hope that you can see a better future ahead so you hold on. Wherever you find yourself at this moment, I want you to know that Jesus is the real answer and the best reason. He is the Author and the Perfecter of your story and of mine. We can thrive in His love. We can choose love in our relationships.

We don't have to take things personally.

I hope these chapters encourage and inspire you to receive God's love and to love others. Read on. You won't regret it.

Love,

Allison

“When you decide to live the God Adventure, you can’t play it safe.”

Love In Action

Many times my marriage didn't feel as if it was thriving, instead it felt as though it was barely surviving. Though we'd go to counseling and read books, we'd still engage in harmful cycles. Jeff and I would have intense confrontations, standoffs, and fighting matches, yet as hurtful as those things were, the cycle continued, no matter the pain. Like cancer, cycles like these can threaten to destroy, but God is the great Healer and Restorer! Because of Him, in every rough relationship, one or both people can take the steps necessary to allow the miraculous to happen. There is no magic formula, but there is one constant answer to our relationship questions. It's found in God's Word. It tells us, "Love never fails" (1 Corinthians 13:8a). This truth points to Jesus. He can help us persevere and choose love, regardless of how messy things get.

God pursues us with His unconditional love. No matter how messed up and lost we are, He still chases us. 1 John 4:8 says: "...God is love." This means that Love Himself is always pursuing you! Not only does He pursue you, but He also wants you to pursue others with His love. It sounds simple, but it's not easy. This is the gospel message. It is why Jesus came. It is our purpose. We were made for relationships, and we were created for community. When we encounter His love, it allows us to see who we really are. It allows us to tell others who they really are. Did you know that love has a language? It speaks of faith and promise. It shares grace and hope. It talks about Jesus.

When I realized that I may be the only Jesus someone ever meets, it shook me! For many years, I over-complicated loving people like Jesus, but I finally stopped trying to figure it out and just focused on living it out. Love in action! You see, Jesus loved us enough to leave heaven for our sake and come to Earth to save us from our sin. Our Father God pursues and pardons us. The Holy Spirit is faithful to interact and fellowship with us. As I've experienced all this goodness and kindness in my relationship with the triune God, I long for others to encounter it as well. I'm motivated by love.

Love is not afraid of a mess. God's love allows us to be real, honest, transparent, and vulnerable, and that will get messy in relationships. But, where there is love, there is no fear. Of course, none of us can love others perfectly, yet here is the most astonishing truth: There is nothing we can do, whether good or bad, to change God's love for us! He simply loves. Everyone strikes out sometimes. The secret is to not stop swinging. You were created to love and be loved! So, when someone makes a huge mistake and hurts you, don't run from them, run to them. When you do, you are being like our Father God! Like Jesus! Like the Holy Spirit!

Love in action is easy to talk about, write about, sing about, blog about and read about, but it takes guts to act out! A kind word, a gentle hug, a smile…these are some simple gestures that communicate love and go a long way. These are examples of love in action, grace on the ground, heaven invading earth! If we only did what was comfortable, we would never need help from the Holy Spirit, our Comforter, Advocate, and Counselor. Living this way requires dependence on Him, and it's what I call the "God Adventure."

When you decide to live the God Adventure, you can't play it safe. The dictionary definition of adventure is "an unusual and exciting, typically hazardous, experience or activity." Choosing to have a God Adventure mindset means that what typically could be hazardous becomes, with help from the Holy Spirit, unusual and exciting. It is living out our faith as we engage in our relationships, and it takes practice. When we commit to living this way, we will be transformed, going from faith to faith and glory to glory! Our Father God designed us for growth. He doesn't want us stuck in unhealthy, destructive cycles in our relationships. So, personally, I am challenging myself to love bigger! Love anyway! I'm looking for opportunities to love within the relationships God has for me. How about you? Will you join me? When we love this way, we don't have to take things personally. We can trust God in the midst of any pain, sorrow, and frustration we may face…because love never fails. God is love, and real love knocks the hell out of you!

"The question you must ask yourself is:

What role do I play in my story?"

ROUND

2

Victim, Volunteer, or Victor?

Have you ever had thoughts like these?: "I can't believe this is happening." "Why me?" "I don't know if I can do this anymore." "I am about to lose it!" "What about me?" Even if you have never said these things out loud, chances are you have thought and felt them. Feelings of inadequacy, brokenness, despair, hopelessness, anxiety and insecurity are the culprits behind these thoughts. Perhaps, you've experienced times when you feel like the whole world is caving in around you, where absolutely everything that could go wrong, does, in fact, go wrong! I've been there. You're not alone! And the truth is, everyone has a story to tell out of their pain. The question you must ask yourself is: What role do I play in my story?

Are you a victim, volunteer, or victor? It all comes down to how you think.

If you possess a victim mentality, then you will always blame someone else for what you're going through. Victims live in a place without peace, constantly deflecting and deeply dissatisfied with life, people, jobs, and things. You can believe in Jesus yet still have a victim mentality because you're not focused on Jesus. I'm not saying that sometimes, though we are completely innocent, we suffer evil at the hands of others. Let me say, if this is you, I'm deeply sorry. Please know that your Father God knows all that you're going through, and He's with you in it. You haven't been left alone to "get over it." Jesus also suffered greatly and unfairly. He never, however, took on a victim mindset, though if anyone ever had a right to, it was Him. If you're struggling as a victim, allow Him to free you from that mindset, so you can get on with the business of healing and living.

When you move about life as a victim, nothing will seem to ever be enough. Those with victim mentalities believe that they are entitled and yet they forget to be grateful. I went through a season when I fell into a victim mentality. I walked around with the attitude that I was a casualty of the actions of others. I became blind to the good things around me because I was so focused on my pain and on what was broken. I forgot to be thankful for my healthy children, my home, family, friends, etc. Finally, when I began to have an attitude of gratitude, my entire mindset began to shift.

To fight against an invasion of a victim mentality, you must take an honest evaluation of your life and relationships regularly. Then, refuse to have a victim mindset which puts the sole blame for your unhappiness or unfulfillment onto someone else. Blame can seem like a way of escape, but it only enslaves you. Blame will tell you that you don't have to take responsibility for how you move forward. It gives the keys of your freedom to someone else.

Instead, if you're stuck in the blame game, ask Father God for help. He hasn't abandoned you. He is with you! And, He is not limited to the things that you and I can see. God can help you believe beyond the realm of what you think is possible and into the miraculous, and He can help you not focus on the pain. No vice, no thing, no person–nothing–can release you from thinking and living like a victim other than your Father God. There is no other way! God wants to help you escape the victim mentality, recognize the good, and live as a victor. Ask Him for help, and then trust Him to do it. Whatever or whomever you trust is what becomes your master. Allow Him to be your Master, and He will help you master your victim mentality. His will for you is to live an abundant life.

If you have a volunteer mentality, you believe that any negative interaction is a result of you. You don't have the right perspective of the situation and allow others to share the blame. Instead, you take the blame solely upon yourself because your identity is wrapped up in what you do or don't do for other people.

Another way the volunteer mindset can play out is by voluntarily putting yourself in situations that are not good for you. What accompanies this mindset is making decisions that you know will have negative consequences but choosing to go through with them anyway. Then, when the "stuff" hits the fan, you think to yourself with pride, "I got myself into this, I can get myself out."

An illustration of this that I can draw from my own life was when I was very young and learning to ride a bike. My parents had warned me to not ride down the hill in front of our home. I thought I was big and skilled enough and that they had no idea what they were talking about. So, when they went back inside the house, I volunteered myself to test out the hill on the bike. As you can only imagine, the story did not end well. I endured plenty of scratches and bruises, yet I so desperately wanted to act as if I was fine. I tried to jump up off the ground, retrieve the bike, and pretend as if nothing had happened. However, I had made a painful mess of myself and the bike, and there was no hiding it. Thankfully, my parents were merciful. Dad fixed the bike, and my mom bandaged my wounds. Still, I had a terrible feeling in the pit of my stomach knowing that I had chosen to do something wrong. I volunteered myself for pain that day. As I have gotten older, I wish I could say that was the only time in life when I knew not to do something but did it anyway. Instead, this scenario has played itself out in many forms throughout the years. I am just so thankful that my Father God has been merciful to me. He has been faithful to bandage my wounds and help me heal.

Having a victor mentality means that you understand the upheaval that has happened in the context of a relationship. Often the upheaval is a result of choices that both you and the other person have made. Yet, because God's Word is true, you embrace Romans 8:28, "And we know that in all things God works for the good of those who love him, who have been called according to his purpose." Victors know that they have already won because of Jesus. They understand that Jesus is everything, and because of Him, they have been made victorious.

In order to have a victor mentality, you have to take a hard look at what you are thinking, feeling, and doing. This means choosing to take responsibility for yourself and also having the right perspective on the role the other person has played in the conflict. Gianna Jessen learned to do this as a teenager. It was then she learned the truth about her life. Before she was born, her 17-year-old birthmother tried to end her pregnancy with Gianna by having a saline abortion. Despite the efforts of others to kill her, Gianna miraculously survived and was born at seven months, weighing just two and a half pounds. She began her life in great physical pain at an abortion clinic, was transferred to a hospital for three months, put into foster care, and finally adopted at age four. Gianna has battled with cerebral palsy her whole life as a result of the decision made by her birthmother that day. No one would argue that she wasn't a victim. In her case, as an unborn baby, she played no part in the offense against her! Yet, she lives as a victor. It's been a journey, of course, but Gianna lives with purpose and joy as she travels the world telling her story and educating people on the horrors of abortion and the redemption found in Jesus.

It can be hard to look at yourself and your relationships honestly, but in order to free the captive, you must first name what is in captivity. So, right now, give your thought life some thought! What mentality are you living in? Wrong thinking leads to problems and not solutions. Here are a few questions to ask yourself:

- Do I let my circumstances and environment set my state of mind, affect my emotions, and direct my actions?
- Do I believe that people can really be transformed by the Word of God?
- Do I let eternity direct my actions?
- Do I believe that I have a divine destiny?

The way you think about things is what forms your habits, which forms your character, which forms your destiny. When you tap into your divine destiny, there will be a deep sense of fulfillment attached to it. You will live with boldness and passion. But if you don't know why you are here, you will be frustrated, destructive, critical, and bored. As a result, your relationships will suffer. There is no limit to the amount of greatness God can do through you. Will you trust Him with your relationships? Ask Him to help you have the right mindset about yourself, people, and situations. You won't do it perfectly, but you can partner with God and do your best. I have learned that when I try, I don't lose. I either win or learn. Failure is part of the process, and people who are always avoiding the fear of failing are also avoiding success.

One of the first mistakes we all tend to make is listening to the enemy instead of listening to God. Too often, we partner with inferior thoughts, which are counter to all the beautiful things God has to say about us. You choose who and what you lean into. You must filter everything through God's Word.

When you're going through a difficult time with someone, remember: Disappointments will last for seasons, but our relationships last a lifetime. Don't get stuck in a season of disappointment. A season is a season. It's not a life sentence. Stay faith-focused with your eyes on eternity. Choose love, choose forgiveness, choose mercy, choose peace, choose hope. It is all a choice. Give yourself and all others the room to be human. Accept the fact that nobody is perfect and even the greatest people will fail you at times. Being human is what binds us all together. We are all on the same team.

When we choose to not let our flesh lead us, but yield to the Holy Spirit, we will not take things personally anymore. You may have struggled in your relationships for years; you may feel that nothing has ever worked out for you. There may even be people in your life who have told you that your situation is hopeless, but it will get better. Stay the course. Partner with what God says about you and your future, and let that fill your thoughts.

“I have learned that when I try, I don’t lose. I either win or learn.”

Jesus First

Making and keeping Jesus first in our life puts our other relationships in their place. I have chosen over and over again for Jesus to be my first love. My relationship with Him is the most important of all my relationships. Keeping this focus has not been as easy as it may sound, but I've had encouragement and examples along the way. My father wisely told me, "God is not at the top of the list, He IS the list!" My hope and prayer is that I will continue to keep Him my first love until the day that I am consumed by His presence and taken into Glory. As I make that my goal, I try to be careful to keep things in check.

Here are a few "signs" that show me that I am in love with God first and foremost, above any other:

1. ***When I make spending time with Him my number one priority.*** I allow Him to captivate my heart over and over as I sit and listen to His voice or read His Word. I may spend my time with Him in prayer or in worship. Sometimes I just sit there and weep or even laugh, but I'm there with Him. Me and Him. Just the two of us.

2. ***When I accept that His desires are more important than my own.*** I realize that what He desires for me is exceedingly, abundantly, above, and beyond what I can ask, think, and imagine. His ways are much better than my own.

3. ***When I believe that what He says about me is more important than any other words spoken about me.*** I walk in the security of His love and not the labels that others, the enemy, or I have placed on myself.

Relationships can be challenging. They can stir up negative things in us that we then have to address, so they don't take over. For example, are you in a relationship that causes you anxiety? The Apostle Paul wrote about anxiety, saying we're not to let it enter us. "Be anxious for nothing…" (Philippians 4:6). If you're a Jesus-follower, then there is no place for anxiety in your life–no matter the situation. Paul goes on to say in that same verse, "...but in every situation, by prayer and petition, with thanksgiving, present your requests to God." Give your affection and attention to God, and anxiety will dissipate. Worrying and being anxious is giving the attention that God deserves to something that is inferior to Him. Everything and everyone is inferior to Him.

Do you understand that there is a battle going on around you? Satan wants you to live in conflict and chaos. Life throws things your way that are too heavy for you to carry alone, but you have the choice to lay down your heavy loads at Jesus' feet and receive His unconditional love, peace, joy, hope, fulfillment, forgiveness, empowerment, desires, sound mind, and a heart to obey. When you give up trying to control your life and the lives of those around you, you will become less anxious and more like Jesus. Actually, becoming nothing is becoming everything.

Jesus shows us in John 14:10 that we must only do and say what the Father is doing and saying. We must be in the Word and spend time in prayer to know what He is saying to us! It is really hard to grasp that He is all we need when we let our feelings and opinions dictate and direct us.

The Father is always accessible! We think that we have to try to enter God's presence when the Scriptures show us that we are always in it. That means there is never a time that He is not with us. There is never a time that He is not for us. There is never a time that He is not loving us and wanting to direct us. David said, "...If I make my bed in the depths, You are there" (Psalm 139:8). We must understand that it is not about an effort to get into His presence, but a choice to recognize and be aware of His presence. This realization transforms us and helps us to walk in the power and authority that Jesus has given us through His name. Keeping this in mind helps us navigate our relationships.

Knowing what I have access to has allowed me to be honest in all areas of my life–both with myself and with others. It also makes room in my life, so that what is happening on the outside does not have to match what is going on inside me. On the outside, all hell can be breaking loose, but on the inside, I am able to experience peace! We all have shattered images and broken places, but in Jesus there is wholeness. In His Presence and gift of restoration, our brokenness and mistakes become lovely masterpieces.

It is important to take a hard look at the places deep inside of you that are ugly. Make yourself vulnerable, so the Holy Spirit can comfort and counsel you. I have walked a very tough road. I've got issues, you have issues, all God's children have issues. Yet, He has equipped us for His good works and pleasure. We are a beautiful, dysfunctional faith family! Knowing this should help you not want to hide the dark places. God's best for your life is not one of surviving but one of flourishing. When we are self-sufficient, we neglect our alone time with Him, and we miss out. But when we meet with Him and make ourselves vulnerable, He guides us. "You make known to me the path of life; you fill me with joy in your presence and with eternal pleasures at your right hand" (Psalm 16:11). What an exciting promise!

God's love has no hidden agendas. He loves because He is Love. If you are a Jesus-follower then you can make the decision to allow love to flow through you into your relationships. The good news is there is an infinite supply, and you won't run out. Partner with God's love. When you do–ready or not–the breakthrough will come! So, don't be afraid when He calls you to step into a new level of your destiny and put love in action for the benefit of someone who has wounded you. This is your time. Just keep your eyes on Him. It is time to push through. When you feel that you are being pushed past your capacity, you are actually creating room for the breakthrough. God makes miracles out of messes and mistakes. What the enemy meant to destroy was only meant to develop you. You were made for this. God is with you. Keep Him your first love.

“Actually, becoming nothing is becoming everything.”

ROUND

4

Heart Eyes

Why don't we just walk away? When we are in a difficult relationship, why don't we just pick up and leave? After all, we live in a disposable culture. We get rid of outdated clothes, used containers, old vehicles...the idea that if something no longer serves its purpose for us, we can simply dispose of it, is a cultural norm. We can easily toss it out and get a different something that is "new and improved." We can start over. We do this with so many things, including relationships, but relationships were not meant to be thrown away or abandoned. I believe in the military term, "No man or woman left behind." We must commit and fight for our relationships.

This is where having "heart eyes" comes in. Using your heart eyes will help you see and remember that the person you're having issues with may not have intended to act, react, or respond the way they did. There is power in remembrance. Remember that you genuinely care for the person you're struggling with and their well-being, even though they've hurt you. Also, remember your own shortcomings. God never throws us out when we fall short. Actually, He calls us closer. He loves.

When my husband had an affair that I knew others knew about, I had to remember that I wasn't ashamed to be seen with him in public before his offense. I had to choose to move forward in love no matter what others were saying or thinking. These are things that you must remind yourself of when you are hurt, ashamed, and angry. It is in these moments that we have to use our heart vision to see the truth that God is working miracles in our lives. Because of that truth, we can have courage and stick with a relationship instead of disposing of it. We can pray Ephesians 1:16-18 over the person: "I have not stopped giving thanks for you, remembering you in my prayers. I keep asking that the God of our Lord Jesus Christ, the glorious Father, may give you the Spirit of wisdom and revelation, so that you may know him better. I pray that the eyes of your heart may be enlightened in order that you may know the hope to which he has called you..."

It is so important that you see the person and the situation you're in with the eyes of God's heart in you. It's not enough to just have our heads involved, but we must have our hearts intimately involved. If we are only led by our heads, our life will be in constant turmoil. We know that sight is a function of the flesh and vision is a function of the heart. When we walk into a room, we may all see the same things, but we will interpret them not through our eyesight but through our heart sight. We must hide the Word in our hearts so that when we look at our circumstances through the filter of the Word, we see what God sees. This causes our heart eyes to be focused and clear.

It's also important to give others sight into who we are and what we are going through because we all need the support. Stop living a double life and keeping things hidden. When my friend, Cathy, finally confided in a pastor at her church about what she was going through with her prodigal son, a weight was lifted from her. She had been sad and ashamed of her son's choices, so she avoided people who might ask questions about him. She kept her pain to herself, so she could maintain the façade that everything was okay, yet she became exhausted by the charade and the fear she felt over others finding out how bad the situation had become. The day she opened up to her pastor friend, she not only gained a prayer partner, but she was released from living under the fear of what others would think and say. Her friend even shared her own pain over her daughter's choices, and they discovered they had more in common than they realized!

Vulnerability invites vulnerability. It takes guts to take the mask off. It takes guts to tell someone, "Look, this is who I really am and what I'm going through, I'm full of pain, or I'm dealing with addictions or abuse, etc." But when we share our brokenness with others, amazing things happen. The people around us are like, "You, too?" and they take off their masks! Remember, we are only as sick as our secrets, and sin grows best in the dark. If you are the only one who knows your secrets, you are in trouble. Your heart has a blockage that needs to be cleared out by the Holy Spirit. The only way to find this freedom is to intimately know God and be intimately known by the people around you. The Bible says that when we confess our stuff to each other and pray, healing happens. "Therefore confess your sins to each other and pray for each other so that you may be healed. The prayer of a righteous person is powerful and effective" (James 5:16). This doesn't give us a license to gossip about the person who has offended us. It points to our own issues.

In my situation with my husband, I came to know that I had to be transformed first before my situation would change and I could live victoriously. I had to deal with the insecurity inside myself before I dealt with insecurity from how someone else made me feel. Insecurity will cause you to believe lies and take the actions of others as personal attacks. When you are secure in who you are, you know the attacks are not personal. Oftentimes, it's actually a reflection of how the other person feels about him or herself. Therefore, in my case, I decided that my circumstances would not determine the way I thought about myself. I needed to use my heart eyes to see myself as Jesus sees me. I also knew that the Holy Spirit could transform people. He could transform me, and He could transform my husband and our relationship. When I got to this place, my life was full of promise–the promise found in Jeremiah 29:11: "'For I know the plans I have for you,' declares the Lord, 'plans to prosper you and not to harm you, plans to give you a hope and a future'."

Our attitude and actions have to come from our hearts and not our heads. That can happen as we cling to Scripture. I know it is so hard to see correctly when you have struggled for years in one or more relationships. It is hard to see hope when you feel as if you are a victim and that others seem to never want the same things you do. So, look to the Word.

I made a choice to let my heart vision come from what the Word said. I decided to be intentional and not be inconvenienced by the way I let God's love flow through me. This type of love says "don't take it personally" when a wrong has been done to us. It chooses to offer hope to the one who hurt us when all seems lost. Be the one who stays and stands. The one who leans in. This is God's way. The more I learn about Jesus, the less I care about anything the world has to offer. God's plans always involve people. This means, if I have His heart, I will desire connection with others. My desire and aim are to be like Him, love like Him, and serve like Him. I don't want to settle for the world's cheap versions of legacy and love. I don't want to toss out what God has plans to restore.

> “What the enemy meant to destroy was only meant to develop you.”

ROUND 5

Forgiveness and Seeds

In addition to all the hurt we've gone through, my husband and I have a very powerful forgiveness story. I can't document the countless times Jeff and I have had difficult conversations that have completely knocked the breath out of me. There have been moments when I thought I would have a heart attack from the pain of his words. During those times, the presence of the enemy was so evident that my home went from being a safe haven to a dangerous war zone. Over and over again, I would endure Jeff's confessions of breaking our covenant, followed by the nauseating thought that my life was ruined. Yet, in the middle of all those intense thoughts and feelings, I'd also experience God's peace while the storm was raging. In those moments, I'd understand that Jesus is all I need. From there, by the power of the Holy Spirit, I was able to not only forgive my husband but to pray for him; though he would break every promise. Through God's amazing grace, I've been given the ability to see Jeff through the eyes of heaven instead of the eyes of hurt, and that led to forgiveness.

As much as my husband's confessions threatened to annihilate me, I knew that only in truth could freedom come. Still, I'd pray (and continue to pray) that this offense would be the last one. No more secrets or infidelity! As I'd pray, I'd hear God tell me time and again, "Fight for him and not with him." Today that is still my mandate from the Holy Spirit as Jeff's wife. Everyone's mandate is different, but that's mine, and I've found that there is no peace like the one that comes from obeying the voice of our Father God. Forgiveness is also an act of obedience.

In this journey, I've learned that the saying "hurting people hurt people" is true. Equally true is this: Healed people heal people. At times, I have been both hurt in some areas and healed in others, yet the only way to have all the hurt places healed is by choosing to stay on the operating table of God (also known as the altar). I know I must remain on the altar for continued healing. It's a process. If you are reading this and have hurt someone, Jesus loves you and forgives you. Your best is yet to come. You have to determine that your present and future will be different from your past, and you must let your past go. If you are reading this and have been deeply hurt by someone, Jesus loves you and has never not been there with you. Hurting people do not intend to destroy their marriages, families, ministries, communities, etc. The enemy, however, takes our weak spots and does all he can to turn them into weapons of death and destruction. When you realize that what someone does that hurts you is not personal and you are not alone, it will change the way you fight. You will not fight with feelings, but you will begin to fight the good fight with faith. Using the weapons that God has given you for tearing down strongholds and rebuilding broken places is your most powerful defense. Stand (and fight) on the promises of God.

Many times the things we are dealing with within ourselves or with others started way before we even understood what was going on. There may have been seeds of perversion from abuse or seeds of abandonment from rejection. There are all sorts of seeds of trauma that exist in this fallen world. These seeds planted in us or in someone we love take root at some point. As a result, sometimes years later, destructive fruit is produced and it infiltrates relationships. This is part of the story of my marriage. Some of the "bad fruit" was able to be picked off through counseling and sheer willpower, but what we came to realize is that the roots of the issues needed to be dug up and burned on our Father God's altar of love. We had to allow the Holy Spirit to do heart (or, "root") surgery, but we still struggled at times and do to this day. The chaotic cycle due, in part, to past trauma and wrong choices, forms fresh roots and they must be dealt with regularly.

If this is you, there is hope. Truth is always the answer. I pray that as you are reading this, the Holy Spirit is bringing things to the surface for you. I hope you are beginning to recognize any dangerous seeds and attacks of the enemy in your life. Have the guts to look at those secrets that feel deep and dark. It is time to get real with yourself and deal with the devil. The fight is actually not with each other, but it is a spiritual battle. So look and see what has been buried and hidden. It's that thing that takes over your thoughts, compels you to act on them, and brings destruction. Offer to the Lord this wise, brave prayer, and He will answer you: "Search me, God, and know my heart;

test me and know my anxious thoughts. See if there is any offensive way in me, and lead me in the way everlasting" (Psalm 139:23-24).

Friend, Jesus' love knows no limits. He is not intimidated by brokenness or sin. He is never shocked. His love constantly pursues you. His love transforms you and how you love others. It is important for me to say that, just because you love Jesus, you won't deal with strongholds. You will because you're not in heaven yet!

If we really live the Jesus way, then we know that we have been given power and authority, but so many of us still live defeated. Jesus shows us and tells us that we have dominion. He says to cast out demons in His name. Remember there is a difference between casting out people and casting out demons. In Mark chapter one, we see Jesus dealing with strongholds. As you read this you will see that Jesus dealt with the evil spirit and not the man. He did not bring destruction to those around him, He brought deliverance. I must choose in my marriage and ministry to bring deliverance through Jesus' name and not destruction. It means choosing to be Spirit-led and Word-fed instead of feelings-led. Don't be consumed by these situations. I know it can be tough to face hard things, but God will help you. Begin to be thankful. You have a purpose, hope, and future! Thankfulness refocuses us from the ashes of our past to the potential of our present and the purpose of our promise.

We see many times that Jesus was preaching and expelling demons as an ordinary part of His ministry. Many times this happened in the synagogues with regular people who worked hard, had families, dealt with certain hang-ups...people like you and me. Don't be fooled into thinking only criminals and maniacs need deliverance and freedom. Many times it's the person looking back at us in the mirror! We all need Jesus. A hang-up can manifest itself in your physical desires, emotions, or mind where there is a cycle of losing control. Therefore, if you or someone close to you has had some continual hang-ups, there is good news: They can be hung up! In the New Testament, everyone who was sent out to share the Gospel was always first commissioned to deal with evil spirits in the name of Jesus. In Matthew 10:1-6, the first twelve disciples were given power over unclean spirits and the power to heal. In Luke 10, Jesus appoints the seventy and commissions them. Today, Jesus has commanded that you and I go and do likewise.

Here is the secret that my mom shared with me: "You can't cast out a demon that you like entertaining." We have to get to a place where our desire for Jesus is greater than our own fleshly desires. The enemy has two main assignments. The first is to keep you from knowing Jesus Christ as Savior. If the enemy fails at this, the next step is to keep you from serving Jesus Christ effectively. The remedy for the flesh is always the cross (Galatians 5:24 says, "Those who belong to Christ Jesus have crucified the flesh with its passions and desires."), but the remedy for demons is to expel them.

If you are a Christian who reads the Bible and prays yet you still have some kind of "special" problem, tormenting issue, or enslaving cycle that seems to always come back no matter how many times you have tried to overcome it, you can be almost sure that you are dealing with a demonic stronghold. It's a death seed, a dark root in the heart. For years, my husband felt that he was flawed. He believed that other people could live free but not him–he felt as if he was forever stuck. This is such a lie of the enemy. We are not defined by our flaws. It is important to understand that willpower alone doesn't work. We need the love and power of God to break strongholds.

After many years of the destructive cycle continuing in my marriage, I asked the Holy Spirit to help me know what to pray, what to ask, and how to respond. Some days I did really well, but other days the sailor's mouth in me came out! Sometimes it seemed as if I had a double personality. It was during this time that the Holy Spirit told me to love my husband unconditionally and to not take any of his offenses personally. How do you not take a thing as painful as infidelity personally? It was when I realized that my husband was the one truly being tormented. He was the one who, despite his greatest natural efforts, could not break free. He was oppressed by the enemy.

As a young man, Jeff experienced abuse that would alter his identity and thought process. Jeff had seeds of perversion, lies, abuse, and self-loathing planted inside him. He did not ask for or deserve these things, but they became part of his broken identity and were brought into our relationship. I remember at one point, while we were having a heart-to-heart conversation, he told me, "I have had this secret with me way before we had each other." It was in this moment that I understood our fight was not with each other. I quit taking it personally and began to pray for Jeff differently. I knew that the fight was within himself.

“Our attitude and actions have to come from our hearts and not our heads.”

ROUND 6

Check The Fruit

Jeff and I met when I was fourteen and he was fifteen. I didn't know his name or anything about him, but I was a young woman in love with Jesus when I walked past a high school concession stand and heard the voice of the Lord say, "That is your husband." Immediately I was thankful that Jeff was good-looking! (Can I get an amen?) From the outside, we looked like we had a fairytale relationship, but there were broken places in Jeff that he was unaware of and I would not understand until later. Early in our marriage, issues began to surface and unhealthy cycles developed. Little did we know they would go on for what seemed like a lifetime, yet I knew that Jeff loved me the best he knew how.

He would ask me after years of infidelity, "How can I make you feel loved?" I would ask him the same question and he would answer, "Your love is unconditional. You see me by faith and are always there for me and with me." My response to his question was sad for him but true.

"I don't get my love from you, I get it from Jesus." Because Jesus is my first love, it made loving Jeff possible when it should have been humanly and emotionally impossible. I also knew that my Father God had said to me that Jeff was my husband, and God doesn't change His mind, even when we change ours. (I continually work to keep His thoughts alive in me and get rid of my own.) I knew that God wanted Jeff to be free, so I asked Jesus to help me to be able to walk with Jeff into his free life.

Thankfully, together, my husband and I decided it was time to do a heart and fruit check. We had some work to do and are still doing it, like casting out and expelling the enemy and disciplining the flesh. Pastor and theologian Jack Hayford says, "You can't disciple a demon and you can't cast out the flesh." Jeff and I realized we were dealing with evil spirits.

There are some signs to look for which will let you know if you are dealing with evil spirits in a relationship or multiple relationships. Evil spirits often entice people to do evil by way of their own thoughts or through the words of someone else. We see this when the enemy spoke to Eve in the Garden of Eden. In this case, he spoke through a snake! He put doubt in Eve's mind by questioning her with, "Did God really say..?" Maybe someone in your life has said things like: "No one will ever know," or "You deserve this," or "Everyone does it; it's not that big of a deal." It may be a voice from someone in your office, someone who just happens to bump into you, or a "friend," but don't be fooled. Behind those voices are evil spirits enticing you.

Evil spirits always harass and torment. They study you and follow you. The Bible is clear about this. It tells us, "Be alert and of sober mind. Your enemy the devil prowls around like a roaring lion looking for someone to devour" (1 Peter 5:8). Many times these attacks come to us in the form of rough days, victim mentality moments, outbursts of anger, resentment, unforgiveness, lust, and the list goes on. You may know of someone whom you know loves their spouse and children, but when evil spirits influenced them and were allowed to have their way in that person's life, all hell broke loose.

The person made their own life and the lives of those they love miserable because they lost the battle. Remember, none of us wrestle against flesh and blood but against spiritual principalities and powers. What follows next is a cycle of shame, remorsefulness, and confusion about why they keep doing what they do!

The torment can also manifest itself physically, emotionally, and/or mentally in addition to spiritually. Unforgiveness is a major door opener for this.

Evil spirits always show up in compulsive behaviors. Maybe you've experienced this yourself. Have you ever thought, "I just couldn't stop myself"? You thought that you had to have it, eat it, drink it, say it, or do it! Personally, my temptation is saying what doesn't need to be said. I'm learning to resist the devil in this area and surrender my tongue to the Holy Spirit. I try to remind myself that I don't have to say what I am feeling or thinking. If what I want to say is going to bring death, it does not need to leave my mouth. End of discussion!

This doesn't mean I should never express myself. It means I must watch how and when I respond and how I talk about certain situations. I sincerely want to speak truth from a place of love, not from a place of anger. How about you? Can you identify where evil spirits may be tempting and attacking you? Pray against them, and ask the Holy Spirit to help you.

We're enslaved by an evil spirit when, though we repent of and receive forgiveness for those sins, we still have the intense desire to commit them. Addictions are formed when we are compelled and enslaved. We can be addicted to television, social media, sex, shopping, substances, attitudes, thought processes, and much more. The bondage may be different, but the binding ropes are the same. Addictions grow frustrations, and we can't just deal with the addiction; we have to deal with the root that causes the bad fruit. Evil spirits are there to defile you. They make you feel dirty and defeated. These strongholds can rise up when you are about to worship and have a breakthrough moment. You must know that all forms of spiritual deception are demonic, and most of the time pride opens the door. They come to weaken and kill. Evil spirits make you restless and want to give up.

There is power in pausing in His Presence. This pause helps us avoid making permanent decisions based on temporary feelings. This pause gets rid of our secrets (which are sacred to Satan) and opens our hearts to freedom. There is no shame, no blame, and no condemnation in God's game. We have to begin to look and see what areas of our hearts are broken. The enemy likes to gang up on us in our emotions. Behind every negative thought and anything that is contrary to the Word of God is an evil spirit. Now, just because you feel something every now and then doesn't mean there is a bad seed planted, but when there is continual bad fruit being produced in your emotions, there is something you need to dig up. Our mind is a battlefield, and we must renew it by the Word of God. "Do not conform to the pattern of this world, but be transformed by the renewing of your mind..." (Romans 12:2a).

One thing that is for sure, when the enemy is at work, lying is always involved. It is important for you to ask yourself, "Do I believe what I am saying? Is this the truth?" When we are living in deception, we don't even realize most of the time when we are lying. We also will lie when there's no reason to. Another thing that happens is the tongue becomes very critical, full of gossip, exaggeration, unclean speech, and negative talk. It's important to be hyper-aware about what you are thinking and talking about. When you use the name of Jesus, all these things will lose their power and influence in your life. Even if you don't know how it all came about, the important part is you do know how to get them out: JESUS. Be humble and honest. You won't face the truth until you first humble yourself to the Word of God. "Humble yourselves, therefore, under God's mighty hand, that he may lift you up in due time" (1 Peter 5:6). When you do, you will produce Godly fruit in your life.

"Forgiveness is also an act of obedience."

ROUND 7

Dignity or Deliverance?

Anytime you are seeking deliverance, you will be confronted with a decision: Do I desire my dignity over my deliverance? If dignity is more important than deliverance, there is a pride problem. For instance, if one of my grandchildren fell into my pool and was drowning while I was stripped down in my bathroom getting ready to take a shower, I would run out butt naked and jump into that pool to save my grandchild because their deliverance is more important than my dignity! It wouldn't matter if a crowd of people would see me in my birthday suit; deliverance is more important! When my husband was drowning in his own sin and shame, many people yelled at him to get out of the water, some even threw life vests, but I jumped in with him and said let's get back on dry ground together. The opinions and gossip of others didn't matter. Deliverance alone was what mattered, and we've walked that journey of deliverance ever since.

The next step to deliverance is confession and repentance. Confession is admitting guilt. Repentance is having sincere remorse for our actions. It also means changing our minds or the way we think. We must change the way we think about sin, about who we are, about who others are, and about who God is. This process of repentance and sanctification is continual for us as believers. "Repent" is not a negative word; it is the greatest gift! It takes us from dark to light. Broken to whole. Shame to acceptance. Shallow to deep. Hell to heaven. Our Father God doesn't want us to confess so He can find out what we've done. He wants us to confess so we can experience His mercy and love. He is never shocked. You can tell Him the worst about yourself. He already knows and still loves you. Be like Jesus–forgive everyone. Even yourself. Then, you'll experience deliverance.

By the way, I know this is a lot, so take a deep breath. Today, you may be the one helping someone in their journey of deliverance, or you may be the one currently in need of deliverance. At some point, we all experience both of these "roles" and often we experience them simultaneously. So now, do a heart check. Think of all the things the Holy Spirit has been bringing to your heart and exhale. Breathe out the things that counter what God says about you, your relationships, and your situation. Now, breathe heaven back in. God is with you.

It is vital we stay in this constant place of exhaling death and breathing in life. Breathe in Jesus. Make Jesus the Lord of every area of your life. Every area

Jesus occupies is safe, and any area He is not Lord over is demonically dangerous. Get your praise on! He has given you "a garment of praise," not "a spirit of despair." (Check out Isaiah 61:3). When you praise the Lord with your life, you bother the enemy and remind him who is in charge. "Submit yourselves, then, to God. Resist the devil, and he will flee from you" (James 4:7). It must be His Word that we live by. Then, deliverance will happen!

The thing is, the enemy wants the consequences of our actions to keep us confused and in bondage. He fights against deliverance. When we make unwise decisions, we pay for them! Yet when things go wrong, we often blame God. For example, when we are overwhelmed with regret, or drowning in debt due to poor spending habits, or we lose our job because we didn't take work seriously, or we experience a broken relationship due to a choice we made, we begin to take these things personally as if God is against us. We must realize that when we have played into the enemy's hand, we will reap the consequences of our bad choices. When we experience things that trigger us to make bad choices, it is important to remember the consequences. Use the reality of consequences as a deterrent. If we think about the consequences of our actions before making decisions, we can limit some bad things from happening. Consequence is a neutral word, but most of the time we think of it in the negative. There are great consequences or rewards for right decisions just like there are bad consequences or penalties for wrong decisions. The enemy always wants to bring negative consequences and make our lives miserable. What dignity is there in that? Don't play into his schemes. Instead, seek deliverance.

When thinking of consequences, I often think of football. My husband was an athlete growing up. So many times, I've found that using sports analogies is an effective way to help us relate in conversation. A football team watches the opposing teams' games on film prior to game time. They study their opponent.

They become fully acquainted with their weaknesses, tendencies, and strong points. The enemy has been assigned to watch your game films. He knows your every move, your sensitivities, your inclinations. He's taken notes and has come up with a strategy to steal, kill, and destroy you. Especially as a believer, the enemy wants to damage and defeat you so that you will live a life of negative consequences. There is a contract out for you and me. It's meant to trip us up and thwart our ability to finish well. But remember, there is a covenant that outweighs that contract. We must learn the schemes of the enemy and stop playing into his hand. In Genesis 3:1 we see a crafty, sneaky, clever, shrewd enemy come in. Satan, appearing in this verse as a serpent, knew how to slither into Eve's life and get her attention. Nothing has changed in our world today. Our enemy, the devil, is still up to no good, and we experience (and suffer) the effects. Like with Eve, he works to fool us into having a conversation with him. We give him our attention, engaging in conversations and meetings with the enemy rather than with the Almighty. We make appointments with a talking, slithering, sneaky snake!

When we look back again at this very first conversation between Satan and a human, we see it was about God. "Did God really say, 'You must not eat from any tree in the garden'?" The enemy references God as Elohim, which acknowledges His power but doesn't include His lordship as it pertains to His relationship with us. The enemy doesn't mind you talking about God, but he's against you having a personal, intimate relationship with God. The enemy is fine with religion. He doesn't even mind you going to church, but He doesn't want you to live a life of heart-to-heart intimacy with your Father God.

The snake itself (the form Satan appeared in the garden) was not a bad creature. Genesis 1:31a tells us that, "God saw all that he had made, and it was very good." God told Adam and Eve they were to rule over the creatures, "Rule over the fish in the sea and the birds in the sky and over every living creature that moves on the ground." Man's relationship with all creatures (including snakes) was initially positive. The enemy has a tactic to use something meant for good and distort God's original design. Isn't that how it works in our lives? We may get off to a good start in life, but if the enemy slithers in and gains a foothold, the good becomes bad. The enemy is great at camouflaging himself so that we can't see him, or we become distracted and don't watch out for him. It would be helpful if we could see plain as day this horrible thing with red horns and a tail and hear his voice speaking to us, but he is very sneaky and even subtle. Satan loves to use something that was created for good and twist it into something bad so that you and I will experience destructive consequences.

The enemy wants you to think that God is holding out on you. Satan didn't talk to Eve about all the freedom that was already hers and Adam's in the garden. The point of the conversation was to have her doubt God's goodness and cause her to focus on the tree they were told they could not eat from. As he conversed with Eve, he painted a false image of God and put His care and best interest for them into question. The enemy will always distort the Word and have us question God's commands or fool us into thinking that they are merely suggestions. Genesis 2:16 says, "The Lord God commanded...," that Adam and Eve not eat from the tree of the knowledge of good and evil. When we dilute God's commands or turn them into suggestions we lessen the impact. Father God's "no's" are so we can enjoy His "yeses." When we eat from the "no" trees we lose the "yes." God's priority for you is freedom. The enemy wants to get you stuck on that one tree so that you can't enjoy the fullness of God's garden. This makes me think of a snotty kid at Christmas. Maybe you know one or have been that kid! After opening presents, he (or she) is surrounded by what looks like a store full of amazing gifts, yet he can't stop thinking about the one toy he wanted but didn't receive. Like this child, perhaps you have lost your heart of gratitude and have taken on a selfish and greedy attitude that is not of God.

Colossians 2:10 tells us "He [Christ] is the head over every power and authority." Therefore, the devil has no power to make you sin, but he suggests sin to you in a multitude of ways. He's a deceiver and because he can't impose sin on you, he wants to mess with your mind. He works to deceive your thought life. If you're not on guard, you will intentionally or carelessly allow him to plant negative thoughts inside your brain. Those thoughts then become your reality as you begin to believe the lies he tells you and who he says you are. From there, your actions are influenced. So, can you see how important it is that you take every thought captive and filter them through the Word of God? God's restrictions enhance freedom! They also bring deliverance.

God was clear to Adam and Eve that they would die if they ate the forbidden fruit, but Genesis 3:4 says, "'You will not certainly die,' the serpent said to the woman." Another one of Satan's common deceptions is that there will be no consequences for our poor choices. What God says is going to happen isn't true. Do not buy that lie! We are so used to lying and changing our minds we think God will too. This is often the strategy the enemy uses, telling us that God's Word cannot be trusted. But God alone is always a truth-teller. Romans 3:4 in the Message version puts it this way: "Depend on it: God keeps his word even when the whole world is lying through its teeth." You can also depend on this: Satan is a liar. In fact, the Bible tells us he is the father of lies. "You belong to your father, the devil...He was a murderer from the beginning, not holding to the truth, for there is no truth in him. When he lies, he speaks his native language, for he is a liar and the father of lies" (John 8:44). The enemy spawns deception, like: "You are not going to die." "This is not going to hurt you." "No one will find out." "You won't get into trouble." "You will not become addicted." "You won't get caught." "You are not going to become emotionally unstable." "It is not going to be that bad." "You're not hurting anyone." And on and on.

What has the father of lies lied about to you? How has that played out in your relationships? Identify the falsehoods, and then have the guts to choose deliverance over (false) dignity regarding any actions you've done while believing the enemy's lies. If someone you love is in need of deliverance, don't take their wrong choices that led to their bondage personally. Instead, help them to identify Satan's lies, and then journey with them toward deliverance and freedom.

“Truth is always the answer.”

ROUND

8

Who Are You Listening To and Focusing On?

We are wise when we take a step back and evaluate who is talking to us and to whom we are listening. Many times, we don't want to have conversations with our Father God because we don't want to answer to anyone, including Him. We can be bad listeners. If we possess a rebellious, stubborn mindset, we are listening to Satan, and we adopt the attitude that says, "No one is going to boss me around or tell me what to do!" We prefer to spend time with and listen to people who are either our equals and/

or people who will validate our experiences. But did you know that you were made in the image of God? This means that you were designed to be dependent on Him. He is "I am who I am" (Exodus 3:14). He is not who or how you want Him to be. He is "I am," and that never changes because God is the same yesterday, today, and forever. It reminds me of teenagers talking as if they are experts in life. "Don't tell me what to do! I know what's best, but I am still expecting you to feed me, clothe me, give me money, drive me, pay for everything…!" We so often want to make choices all on our own but expect God to pay the bill!

The whole point is this: All choices (who we listen to, what we engage in) have consequences. There may be areas in your life right now that are dying or dead because you are not listening to God. Instead, you're eating from the self-sufficiency tree thinking you're your own boss, the one in charge. It reminds me of a story I heard about Mohammad Ali. He was flying on a plane, and the flight attendant asked him to buckle up, but he just sat there, ignoring her request. She asked him politely a few times until finally, he said to her, "Superman doesn't need a seat belt!" To that, she kindly replied, "Superman doesn't need an airplane." What a wise response! The truth is, all of us are passengers in this life, and we need to buckle up with Jesus. We must submit every area of our life to the Holy Spirit and listen to Him.

While the enemy was speaking in Genesis chapter three to Adam and Eve, they began to look through the lens of the enemy, rather than with their God eyes. Satan's view is, "If it feels good, do it." Eve, while in the Garden, had to have passed by the tree of the knowledge of good and evil multiple times, but this time she had a deceptive view. The deception was that she only focused on the "good" this time and not the "evil." She changed her vision to see through the lens of the enemy, Satan.

When we are falling into one of the enemy's traps, our sight becomes skewed and we only see what we think is good and not evil. If we could see ourselves living out the negative consequences first and see ourselves in the broken state in advance, the "good" wouldn't be all that. The enemy wants to erase the ugly evil and make you only see the sparkle. When we are tempted and then fall into his trap, our physical appetite is changed, our emotional appetite is changed (our sinful desires take over), and our intellectual appetite is changed (we think we know it all and are indestructible), but all of this is deception because nothing can rule over the Word of God. When something conflicts with divine revelation, any other "fact" or false truth and feeling is ignorant in comparison. The Word of God calls that foolishness. Proverbs 12:14 says it plain and powerfully: "There is a way that appears to be right, but in the end it leads to death."

Instead, we must listen to, focus on, and desire wisdom. "She [wisdom] is a tree of life to those who take hold of her; those who hold her fast will be blessed" (Proverbs 3:18). We must eat from the Word of God so that we can be discerning. "But solid food is for the mature, who by constant use have trained themselves to distinguish good from evil" (Hebrews 5:14).

Don't be so impressed with what looks impressive, according to the world. Don't be faked out! And, don't live like a fake either. The most attractive quality anyone can have is their love for Jesus. Our body ages, our looks change, and the cosmetics wear off, but we're beautiful in Jesus. A heart surrendered to Christ echoes throughout eternity. He is the only one who fulfills. When you live in Christ Jesus, you are rich beyond measure and have everything necessary to walk through life in His power. So, are you listening to Him or to Satan? Are you fixing your eyes on Jesus or giving your attention to the enemy? Remember, there has never been a time that you have not been fully known, fully seen, and fully loved by Father God. That's the goodness of God! We are wise and victorious when we listen to Him and keep our focus on Him.

We have to know what to ignore and what to ignite. This takes some thought and focus. There are no days off, but the commandment is simple: Love God and love people. Serve God and serve people. You can choose to have comebacks today in every area of your life and in every relationship by praying (which includes listening to God) and praising Him. If your current situation doesn't look like the dream destination, don't give up. Your breakthrough is in transit.

In my journey, as I've listened to my Father God, I've come to know that nothing and no one captivates quite like Jesus. Time with Him is more important than anything else, so I can't encourage you enough to spend time with Him. When you do, you will move from a place of obligation into desire. You will move into a place of wanting to fulfill His desires for your life more than your own desires. Jesus does not give us suggestions; He gives us commands. So I knew, for instance, that Jesus did not suggest that I love and forgive Jeff, He commanded it and expected it. He also gave me the Holy Spirit, so I could do it. And, believe me, I've gotten really good at crying out for His help! The truth is, on our own we do not have the power to overcome the enemy's schemes. Our Father God never meant for us to do it alone. That is why it is beneficial to us that Jesus would send us the Holy Spirit. He is the power source to live free and to live in love! But we must listen and obey.

When I was young, I had these great desires and dreams about what my life was going to look like, but I had to begin to discipline myself to do what the Word said. Desires don't determine your destiny but disciplines do. God is not opinionated; He has a will and a way. God loves us. God forgives us. It is never too late to go His way. We must make decisions for our destiny, not for our temporary desires. Do not make decisions based on how you feel. If what your flesh and feelings tell you to do doesn't line up with what God tells you, they are not what He has for you. Let Him be in control. It reminds me of game systems like Atari, Nintendo, Xbox, and Playstation. One thing all of them have in common is a controller. The same is true in life. No matter how much you upgrade, you will always have a controller, something that is directing you. It is your choice to be Spirit-controlled or sin-controlled. "For the flesh desires what is contrary to the Spirit, and the Spirit what is contrary to the flesh. They are in conflict with each other, so that you are not to do whatever you want" (Galatians 5:17). Ask yourself whether the Spirit or the flesh has been controlling your mind, feelings, conversations, actions, and atmospheres! Who are you listening to and allowing to control you?

Everything you are looking for in life, including in your relationships, can only be found in Jesus. It is not found in people, places, positions, possessions–only Jesus. When you give it all to Him, He will do something that no one else can do for you and you can not do for yourself. Take an honest look at your thoughts, your focus, and what and who you give your attention to. Look deep into your heart and examine it with the help of the Holy Spirit under the scalpel of the Word of God. If you're not listening to Father God and keeping your focus on Him, your heart eyes and ears are listening to and focusing on the wrong thing.

When Jeff and I got married, like so many people, we thought we were leaving the past behind us. That's not to say we don't both have wonderful parents. I grew up in a home that was full of love and focused on Jesus, and Jeff grew up in a home of love, too. However, it wasn't until he was older that both he and his parents truly experienced God's unconditional love. After that, things changed for the better. I believe everyone is genuinely trying to do the best he/she can. Nevertheless, remember, the enemy doesn't fight fair, and he is always looking for ways in and vying for our attention.

After many years of counseling and growth, we both now know that the lessons of our early years formed the decisions we made with one another. The communication skills (or lack of them), the trauma, and the pain of our early years have had a direct impact on our life together. These still influence us today, and we continually have to go to the Word of God and refocus. It is only by the grace and mercy of God that we are together and choosing to continue the good fight of faith. The funny part is, I have been completely in love with Jesus and Jeff nearly my entire life. I actually don't just love Jeff, but I like him most of the time! When we took our wedding vows we meant them. It wasn't until over 20 years of marriage, however, that he realized he was under the influence of familiar evil spirits. Jeff realized that the chord that connected his heart and mind was severed. The Holy Spirit revealed to him that he had hidden his heart as a little boy and never truly dealt with all the brokenness. Even now, if you ask Jeff to talk about his childhood (the good or bad parts), it's hard. It has been very difficult for him to bring up many positive memories from his younger years. His double life of deception began during his farming years as a young man, but I know that when he met me, he also met the real Jesus in me. He asked Jesus to come into his heart and wanted to serve Him, yet there were areas and strongholds that he had never dealt with. The important thing to know is that our Father God is relentless in His pursuit of our hearts. God is faithful to finish the good work that He has begun in us. So why would we want to listen to or follow anyone over Him? He alone can heal and help us.

"There is no shame, no blame and no condemnation in God's game."

Past Impact

After all these years of walking through trauma with my husband and others, I can tell you that if something happened to people in their adolescent years that had a particularly negative effect on them, and they never truly dealt with it, severe cuts in their heart were formed. When this is the case, this secret pain becomes the foundation of how they process every decision and situation without them even being aware of it. Secrets are sacred strongholds to Satan, but Truth sets us free. Lies that are written on our hearts create an unhealthy emotional life. If this is you, you may feel as if you are flawed or even crazy; you may blame yourself and take responsibility for something that is not your fault. But the truth is, you have been attacked by the enemy. (If the devil can't take you out, he will try and wear you out.) You must call him out. Call out the lies, and replace them with truth.

Psychology reveals that trauma causes the brain to malfunction. Trauma can cause you to react instead of respond. Then, you do things and say things that, when you look back, you think, "That's not what I wanted to say or do!" You must take those traumatic thoughts and filter them through the Word of God, so they don't control you. You must see yourself through Jesus and who He says you are and not through the lens of the trauma. This will help you regulate your emotions. It will change the way you process your senses. Also, feelings can be liars. If you listen to those lying messages, it will actually change your mind. This is why renewing your mind with the Word of God is so important. Taking every thought captive and filtering it through faith is essential to retrain your brain to be heavenly-minded.

In our journey, Jeff and I have also learned that life and death are in the power of the tongue, so we made a conscious decision to change our confessions over ourselves and each other. We began to verbalize what the Word of God says instead of what we just felt or thought. We knew that our lives were (and continue to be) shaped by our words, and if we wanted a different life, it was important for us to have different words. Life words. There is something about repeating the promises of God out loud that brings healing and hope.

It is so important that you bring your past under the redemption of the Cross and what Jesus has done. This will shift the way you deal with life. Don't try to bury the trauma, pain, and lies because that never works (more on that later), but instead burn them on God's altar of love. Go to Father God. He will begin to mend those broken places and build a healthy emotional life within you. Then you won't have to give in to fear, cave into temptation, and try and hide with chaotic coping. I'm not saying it's easy, but it's possible with Jesus.

We are all impacted by our past: the things that happened to us and the decisions we made. So, even though Jeff knew God loved him and that I did too, he still had a very hard time receiving it. He had a performance mentality, believing that receiving love and acceptance was based on performance. This way of thinking helped him excel as an athlete and employee/employer, but it caused him to struggle in relationships. It also caused him to believe that if he did not perform to a certain standard, he would not be loved and accepted by Father God. Additionally, he did not think that his voice really mattered, only his performance. After he suffered abuse, his voice and opinion became lost. And because he had done things that he knew were wrong, but found pleasure in them, the enemy would tell him that he would never be able to think right. These are lies, of course, but if you believe a lie it is true to you.

We know that everyone needs to be loved for who they are no matter what they've done. We need to hear those affirming words and actions that tell us we are valued and cherished. We need acceptance and affection. We all need to feel safe, supported, stable, and protected. We need to be heard. We need to be comforted. These are all ways that we experience love! When our emotional and physical needs are not met or even ignored, we often adopt a perverted view of ourselves and our relationships.

At one point, Jeff expressed to me that he had buried his heart. What he was really saying is, "I buried my pain." Pain that is buried doesn't die, it distorts. We had to address the pain. We also had to make a choice toward deliverance by recognizing the good. It helped me to go on a "treasure" hunt. I wanted to see my husband become the man that God gave me in dreams and visions. The man I dreamed of was not broken. We know that everyone has trash and treasure in them, but I chose to be a treasure hunter instead of a trash inspector.

I understand that when you don't receive unconditional love as a child, it's really hard to give it as an adult. But I am fully persuaded that God can take the worst mess and make it into a beautiful message. You see, the heaven happening in you is much greater than the hell happening around you. Your struggle will not become your identity if you believe who Jesus says you are. The devil is a liar, but God is the ultimate truth-teller. And, Jesus is enough. He is with you and He is for you, no matter your past. We all have had our hearts hurt by others or even by ourselves, but we have to make the conscious decision to do the work with Jesus and get healed from any past impact. It's always worth it

“Do I desire my dignity over my deliverance?”

ROUND 10

The Good, the Bad, and the Ugly

God's love is covenantal. It's a love that says, "I will choose you even when you don't deserve it. I will love you through every circumstance. My love for you is relentless and true." When we said our wedding vows, Jeff and I repeated 1 Corinthians 13:1-8. Love is what put Jesus on the cross for you and me. Love is what defeats the enemy. Love is what gives purpose to our future. I'm talking about the type of love that says, "I love you even if you don't love me back." I wanted to love Jeff like this. I actually want to love everyone like this! And, yes, I am a work in progress! I want to have a love that keeps no record of wrongs. This means that I want to love no matter what I feel. Love is not a feeling, it is an action and a person, and His name is Jesus.

Obviously, life is hard and love can be hard, but we were made for hard things. Still, I have really messed up at times. I have struggled in more than one relationship in my life, and I'm guessing you have, too. Ministering to someone when we have messed up doesn't make us a fraud. God still uses us because truth is all about Him, and our struggle doesn't define who we are. If you are going through something right now and thinking thoughts like, "What about me? Don't I deserve to be happy? I am sick of doing what everyone wants me to. I just want to live my life," then you are thinking "rescue me" thoughts. When they form in your mind, take the time to ask yourself some heart questions: "Do I have a cycle in my life I need to break?" "Have I been performing for people?" "Do I have pain that has been buried alive?" "Do I have unforgiveness in me?" Then, go to the Word and allow it to illuminate the issues inside you. If you need help, seek out a mature Christian friend, a Christian counselor, or your pastor, and ask them to go on a treasure hunt with you. Ask the Holy Spirit to direct you and rescue you from wrong thinking. Ask Him to shape your character.

Since I was a young woman, I have always desired for God to work His character in my life. He has given us the ability to cultivate His character through His Spirit. The Bible says: "Have the same mindset as Jesus Christ…" (Philippians 2:5). The word "mindset" also means "attitude." This means we have to make an attitude adjustment to be like Jesus. We have to be transformed by the renewing of our minds. My dad always said, "Your gift or talent will get you in the door, but your character will keep you in the room." Character is foundational. Who we are in private is the true demonstration of our character. If we are living a double life, it doesn't matter who we are in public, our true character will eventually be exposed. What we refuse to deal with now will deal with us later. Our private victories set us up for public triumphs. The gospel, while deeply intimate, is lived out in public. It's lived out in relationships.

God's Word has all the answers for today's problems. The Word is always relevant. Knowing this, I began to turn to the Word of God for direction in my life in every relationship and in every situation. I read everything I could find on forgiveness, love, marriage, divorce, fear, faith, and peace. At the end of the day, I knew I had to always go God's way. If you will allow yourself to process your hurt and pain with the help of the Holy Spirit, great purpose can come from it. These moments with just you and Jesus can be the most beautiful parts of your journey.

Remember God does not cause the broken places in our life. "This is the message we have heard from him and declare to you: God is light; in him there is no darkness at all" (1 John 1:5). Things happen and there are good and bad consequences. I cling to Romans 8:28 which tells us: "And we know that in all things God works for the good of those who love him, who have been called according to his purpose." This isn't saying that all things are good, but it does tell us that God can bring good out of all things. Mistakes don't disqualify us from being loved by God. I am so glad that God doesn't treat the Bible like most people do on social media, only showing the highlights. We are given examples of people who loved and followed God, but we can also read many examples of people messing up, living dysfunctional lives. The good, the bad, and the ugly–at some point and in some form, we experience being all three, but God loves us and can bring good out of our mistakes.

“We have to know what to ignore and what to ignite.”

What Has Gotten into You?

Attitude has a lot to do with the way we choose to think about things around us. Our attitudes also affect all of our decisions and actions. I am thankful that Father God gives examples of broken people with wrong attitudes being used in mighty ways. There are several people in the Bible who had to make attitude adjustments. I think of Joseph in the Bible. (You can read all about him in Genesis, chapters 37-50.) As a boy, he was given dreams from God as he slept, and at first, he had a haughty attitude about them. He bragged about these dreams, which drove his already jealous brothers nuts and fueled their disdain for him. Still, God fulfilled the purpose he had for Joseph's life and, in the process, his attitude was changed. Even though Joseph's brothers sought to get back at him by putting him into a pit, he did not let the pit get into him. He also did not let his experience with Potipher's wife get into him. He did not let prison get into him. He did not let the palace get into him. Instead, he kept the promises of God in him–front and center–and God's purposes were amazingly fulfilled. Many times, we are petty, pitiful, people-full, prison-full, and prideful when we need to be full of promises and purpose. We need to let that shape our attitude and direct our life and relationships.

Maybe as you read this, you are full of wrong attitudes. Maybe you are living a double life. Perhaps you are a prisoner of unforgiveness. Maybe you are drowning in a pit of self-pity. Is people-pleasing your stronghold? Pride may be what continues to trip you up. Whatever kind of "pit" you are in, there is a way out. Are you willing to make the real sacrifices to live free? It is a choice to do whatever it takes no matter the cost...and it will cost you. You have to lay down your own life. To live a transformed life, you have to want freedom more than you want familiarity. You've got to change your attitude.

Allow this truth to get into you and encourage you: No matter what sin you have done or what has been done against you, no matter the amount of pain you have caused or have experienced, God doesn't negate His calling on your life. I know that I have been called to preach the gospel since I was a very little girl and Jesus appeared and spoke to me. Since then, no man can compare to my first love. I tell people that I am still married today to Jeff because I was first married to Jesus. It is hard sometimes for people to understand why someone would fight for something that looks like it is worth nothing, but Jesus has done the same for me. He rebuilds the ruined cities. So no matter your circumstances, know that you are loved. Romans 8 says that there is no condemnation for those who are in Christ Jesus. You are not disqualified from the call of your divine destiny no matter your situation. I believe that in our darkest places God's love light shines the brightest. The truth is if you want to live a whole, healed life you can. If God's Word is true, no matter how far over the edge you have gone, no matter where you find yourself, if you want to be free, you can be. Let that truth get into you and take over your attitude! When you do, it will radically affect your decisions, actions, and relationships.

I personally believe that there is not a more powerful decision you can make in relationships than the one to love people. Love is the most catalytic force on the planet. Making this decision is what has made the marriage that shouldn't have made it a testimony of God's love. It was not one night of prayer, one great conversation, one counseling session, one church service, one God-encounter that transformed our lives, but it was a holy attitude adjustment that brought on one decision that declared, "I am going to choose you, whether or not you choose me." I decided in my heart that I would know God's love personally and that I would walk in that love. My life's goal is that when people meet me they will encounter the love of God through me.

God will lead you into a life of love and into relationships that overflow with love, but the simple truth is that you must fall in love with God first. Jeff and I have a relationship full of love despite the struggles and challenges. We are deeply "in" love. We are best friends. We miss each other when we are apart. We're affectionate with one another. We would have missed out on all this lovin' if we had stayed stuck in the past. It's impossible to walk in your divine destiny when you don't press on and move forward in love with Jesus. It is true we can't have a brand new start, but we can live in a way that gives us a happy ending.

Be careful not to waste your efforts on things that don't have eternal significance. Investing in our relationships is never a waste. We were not designed to find our purpose in control, power, ownership, and positions, but the fulfillment of our life has a lot to do with the quality of our relationships. We are commanded: "Love the Lord your God with all your heart and with all your soul and with all your strength and with all your mind, and Love your neighbor as yourself" (Luke 10:27). This is of utmost importance according to Scripture. We will find satisfaction in our loving relationship with our Father God and in our loving relationships with others when we obey this commandment. The amazing part is that living this way will transform everything. As you grow in your ability to love God, your ability to love others will grow, too. Talk about an attitude adjustment!

Ephesians 3:17-19 tells us that we need to be rooted and grounded in love. Just like wrong roots produce bad fruit, God's roots produce good fruit. There are people we don't want to love and reasons that we may choose to distance ourselves. We can always find a way to justify our lack of love and lack of forgiveness. These reasons or excuses do not bring about heart-healing and develop us emotionally. We lose if we don't love. When we take the mask off, we realize that everyone was created to love and be loved. Love is the root of our spiritual being. God is love and we were created in His love image.

It is empowering when we choose to walk in God's love. It not only empowers us, but it protects us. When this love is evident, our identity can be secure in Him. It is through the Holy Spirit that we are able to walk in sacrificial love. Grace gives us the ability to do things that we cannot do in our own strength, like love someone sacrificially. Love is the secret to a life of faith and power. God's agape love is true love. Agape love includes feelings, but it supersedes human emotions and character. Even though it is sacrificial, you will not lose yourself in agape love; you will only gain and allow others to as well. This love causes you to lay down your life as a bridge for others to experience God. This love found in 1 Corinthians 13 is love in action that represents the nature and character of God. Did you also notice that all the actions of agape love are for the other person? They are for the blessing of someone else, but we are blessed, too. Real love doesn't have a personal agenda. Every time I exercise love in action with Jeff, it is to direct him to a loving God who can meet all of his needs and bring wholeness to his heart. I'm able to do that because of Jesus.

We so often want someone else to take the first step, give us something, or do for us to make amends. Our attitude is, "You go first and maybe I'll respond." We want people to initiate and pursue and do all of the things we want or expect them to do. However, I would challenge you to be the one to love first. Go ahead and value those you are in relationship with.

This love is what empowers us to face our issues and take the masks off. The Bible says that faith works through love. This love stretches us to trust and believe in God more and more. Let God and His love get into you!

It is in those vulnerable dark times that we can make giant leaps forward in love. Leaps that say, "No matter what, I love you!" This has been the case in my marriage. I have never wanted to stay married just for the sake of staying married. I have not wanted our union to ever end in divorce either. I have always desired a flourishing marriage with my husband. Do you desire your marriage, friendship, relationship with a family member, etc. to flourish? If not, recognize any wrong attitude and allow the right one to get into you. Then, you will experience intimacy with God and with others.

It is through continual heart-to-heart communication that our relationships grow stronger. Your acts of love form a net, helping those in relationships with you to feel safe. Communication and heart connection is fertile soil for love to grow in relationships. I encourage you to begin having conversations where you really listen to the other person. There is ministry in your presence. Even though you may not be interested in everything they are saying, be interested in them. This will cause you to lean in and listen with your heart. Love doesn't look to its own needs but considers the needs of others. This is done by paying attention. Isn't it great when someone knows what you are interested in or care about without even asking you to tell them? You know when you get around these people. They are listening to more than your words.

“Secrets are sacred strongholds to Satan, but Truth sets us free.”

ROUND 12

The Real F Word

For me, forgiveness is the real F word. C.S. Lewis wrote, "Everyone says forgiveness is a lovely idea until they have something to forgive..." So true! If you are drowning in pain and wonder how you'll get through this latest hurt, let me ease your mind with this truth: Love covers ALL, and forgiveness is possible. The power of God in you squashes the flesh to let you live out love and forgiveness.

Forgiveness can be so challenging, but by God's grace, I learned the importance of it when I was young. When I was a little girl, one Bible story that stuck with me is when Peter asks Jesus how many times he should forgive someone who has sinned against him. Jesus first replies with what would seem to be an absurd number—"seventy times seven"—and then He explains His answer with a parable about forgiveness. (Check out Matthew 18:21-35.)

Forgiveness works through faith and love. Emotionally healthy people have a deep sense of God's love and have sincere love for others. Dysfunctional behaviors and emotions come from the absence of love or distorted forms of love. When we think about the word love, most people think of it in ways that God does not. Remember that our Father God's love doesn't have a dark side. He is 100% pure. His love is lived in the light. It is important to let people know that regardless of their actions, you are committed to God's agape kind of love toward them. God will help you with that commitment, and that commitment will help you forgive.

The condition of our lives is determined directly by our condition of love. The Word tells us that this is the only true proof of spiritual growth. Paul also says that love coming from a pure heart is the goal. Everyone wants love, but it seems very few of us really experience God's love and share that love with others. Father God is always giving love. It is our choice to receive it and let it flow through us to others.

I have a confession: At times, I wish that I could control others and help them make the right decisions. Of course, I can only control myself and even in that, I need the help of the Holy Spirit! In my situation, though the Lord told me to stay and fight for my family, that didn't mean I could make Jeff do the same. Even today, he has the choice to stay or go. When you are in a broken relationship, you can only do your part. No matter how much I prayed (I believe praying is necessary for our heart posture toward the other person), I still could not change Jeff. He had to personally desire it, and the Holy Spirit had to help him. What I could do was pray the Word of God over him, myself, and our family! Still, things rarely go according to my plans or timetable. Most healing takes time and is not immediate. I had to get to a place where I began to thank God that He would complete the good work He began in us. Yes, there are times the Holy Spirit does do something suddenly, but for me, it has been more gradual. I wish I could say that the healing and restoration in our marriage came quickly, but I will not mislead you. The pace of change has been steady but slow. I like to call it long obedience in the same direction. We have good, bad, happy, and sad days. It's a mixed bag.

The miracle, however, is this: Through it all, there has been peace in the waiting. The joy of the Lord has been my strength, and it can be yours, too. The miracle is that God told me to love Jeff unconditionally, not take stuff personally, and that He would help me do it. And He has! I now know that forgiveness is a supernatural thing that is only possible with the help of the Holy Spirit. It's also part of our God Adventure. Two of the secrets of how Jeff's and my marriage have been able to be sustained are God's unconditional love and His gift of forgiveness.

You may be thinking: "But, what if someone does something that is truly unforgivable?" Scripture does not provide us with a list of forgivable and unforgivable offenses against each other. It just says we are to forgive. This is not a suggestion; it's a command. The great thing is, God never asks us to do anything that He has not equipped us to do. Matthew 18:21-22 makes it clear that we are not only to forgive, but we are to forgive over and over again: "Then Peter came to Jesus and asked, 'Lord, how many times shall I forgive my brother or sister who sins against me? Up to seven times?' Jesus answered, 'I tell you, not seven times, but seventy-seven times'." Forgiveness is serious business.

For many years, Jeff struggled with sex addiction, and I struggled with forgiveness. Now, forgiveness doesn't mean forgetting and acting as nothing happened. It does mean that I am no longer going to hold Jeff responsible for the pain I feel. Forgiveness is freedom. The Bible says to forgive over and over and over again. Until this happened in our marriage, I am not sure that I understood this command. As my mind would run wild, I would have to take those thoughts captive, apply the blood of Jesus, and filter them through God's Word so that I could forgive. Every time you remember something and it causes an emotional reaction, you have to reapply forgiveness. Forgiveness has become my immediate response. I forgive before something needs to be forgiven, but I also seek to apply the wisdom of Proverbs 3:5-6: "Trust in the Lord with all your heart and lean not on your own understanding; in all your ways submit to him and he will make your paths straight." I am supposed to trust Him with all my heart and love people. Now, this may all sound easy, but it was hard getting the "hell" out of my head and the Word in my mouth. I had to choose to be intentional with my thoughts and my words. I realized God has forgiven me more times than I will ever have the opportunity to forgive Jeff or anyone else.

I remember thinking, "Lord, how do you forgive and then forget?" He reminded me that I am to be like Jesus. I wondered, "Does Jesus remember hell?" Yes, I believe He does and even has the scars to prove it, yet His love for me made it worth it to Him. My love for God and others made my hell and the scars worth it. When I look at our scars, I see a future and not a past. Many years ago, the Holy Spirit woke me up and showed me myself on a stage sharing with others how to fight for their family and not with their family. Forgiveness is part of the good fight of faith.

Here is another scripture that has stayed with me, "Be kind and compassionate to one another, forgiving each other, just as in Christ God forgave you" (Ephesians 4:32). All these forgiveness verses became so clear to me. I was equipped with the power of God to forgive! "Therefore, as God's chosen people, holy and dearly loved, clothe yourselves with compassion, kindness, humility, gentleness, and patience. Bear with each other and forgive one another if any of you has a grievance against someone. Forgive as the Lord forgave you" (Colossians 3:12-13).

Forgiveness is not for the other person as much as it is for you. I must receive personal forgiveness from God so that I can set others free of their failures. I believe that most of the ground the enemy gains in a believer's life is because of unforgiveness. We were created for relationships and this is one of the most important places forgiveness is needed. People we love are going to hurt us, and we are going to hurt them. The question is how will we respond when we get hurt? I have already made up my mind that I am going to forgive. It is amazing to me that whatever any of us have done and whatever our motivation is at the time, God forgives us. And He wants and expects us to do the same.

This importance of forgiveness started long ago in a garden. Adam and Eve were unashamed until sin entered their lives and intimacy was broken. This is what unforgiveness does in our lives. It breaks intimacy with God and others. Jeff and I had to let the past hurts and offenses go so that we could gain the ability to love each other as we should. We have had to deal with this issue of forgiveness in order to enjoy real intimacy. Forgiveness is a purifying agent for our lives and relationships. We had to choose not to play the shame and blame game.

So, friend, let it go! It's time! I want to encourage you today to let go of your past and stop looking behind you. Unforgiveness causes us to live in our past rather than our present; it prevents us from moving forward. You have to turn off the replay in your mind and let it all go and God has given you the power to do that. You can choose love! Forgiveness is a choice. Choose to love the person that has offended and hurt you. Then let your behavior and mouth reflect that choice. (Warning: It won't be easy.) This doesn't mean you have to be in an active relationship with them, but you've released forgiveness to them. Decide not to dwell on the past.

Instead, bless them out! My dad has always told me you will never meet anyone God doesn't want to bless. Yes, even those that have hurt you. Remember, hurting people will hurt people. In Luke 6:28, Jesus shows us how to "bless out" those who mistreat us: "bless those who curse you, pray for those who mistreat you." This is a powerful weapon in changing wrong thoughts and negative feelings. Prayer transforms hurt into hope and criticisms into compassion. If you refuse to pray for someone, it shows that you are failing the forgiveness test.

Do not bring hurt into your future. Settle in your mind and heart now that you will always forgive (again and again). Successful relationships are possible if we follow God's lead in love and forgiveness. When you apply these ideas, it will change the atmosphere. I believe in being a thermostat and not a thermometer. Thermostats set the atmosphere and thermometers just read atmospheres. You are an atmosphere changer with God's love.

I am able to love Jeff today because of the miraculous power of forgiveness, which is only available with help from the Holy Spirit. I am so thankful that we chose God's way instead of ours. We chose to not let the past, pain, pride, pettiness, or people stop us from our God-purpose. I am praying that you will choose love and forgiveness today. Here is a simple prayer that I use and I think you'll find it helpful. But when I was in the thick of it, I want you to know that sometimes all I could do was whisper the name of Jesus. And, that was enough.

"Heavenly Father, thank You for loving and forgiving me. Thank You for bringing me into a relationship with You through Your Son Jesus and for showing me love and forgiveness in action. Help me!

Holy Spirit, show me how to share the same forgiveness with others that You have shown me. Put Your super on my natural. Let others see You living in me. In Jesus' name I pray. Amen."

"The heaven happening in you is much greater than the hell happening around you."

Holy Life

I believe that the best is yet to come. I pray that we are going from glory to glory and faith to faith. Glory to glory means less of me and more of Jesus. It's the light of Him shining through me. Faith to faith means increase. You can increase your faith by reminding yourself of the "small" miracles and victories He has helped you to win. These things will encourage you to trust that God has "big" victories in store for you as well. Celebrate and recognize the small. Go treasure hunting, diamond digging...look for the victories! (For example, "I didn't snap at my child this morning before school! Victory!") When you find these "wins," you will live in gratitude and have a hope-filled life. You will be ready for the bigger victories when they come.

As we seek to live a holy life, we must trust God. Know and believe that His Word in us is good. When we trust someone, we believe that they will not let us down, but it really comes down to this: When you are following the Holy Spirit's leading in your life, then I can trust you. You won't let me down, and the Holy Spirit in me won't let you down. Me in me–now that's a different story! When I am being led by my flesh and feelings, I am not always trustworthy and neither are you. In those moments, we become selfish or protective of ourselves. But when we trust God, we ignore every other voice. The voice of the enemy, the voice of ourselves, and the carnal voice of others all must be ignored. The Word says that His sheep will know His voice and that the voice of a stranger they will not follow. Let Him lead you in love today. Pastor and theologian R.C. Sproul said, "Whatever else God's love is, it is holy." Invite holiness in.

So how do you live holy? There is no area in your life where you can be lazy and see gains. You won't see improvement if you are careless, irresponsible, and undisciplined. You must choose to outlast everything. Endurance always has the final word. The way to live a holy life is to be satisfied by God. When you look at Jesus, you won't stare at anyone or anything else. Choose to live in His Presence. Jesus must be your first love. When you set your life apart for God, you are practicing holiness. This does not mean you are perfect. It means you are choosing to conduct your life according to the Word of God and be led by the Spirit of God.

Holiness is choosing to turn away from the ways of the world and live in agreement with God's Word. Holiness is not accidental; it is intentional. It requires a decision of your will. His power in you will transform you from the inside out. Holiness is one of the main keys to happiness.

If you were offered what seems to be the sweetest of sins' pleasures, would the offer make your soul sick because you are so satisfied with Him? The root of all sin is selfishness. Selfish people end up creating broken families, and these families create shattered societies. Each of our lives was splintered because of selfishness in the Garden. We must be committed to Him to live a holy life. We must be committed to Kingdom families. Hold everything earthly with an open hand, but grasp eternal things with all you've got. Ask the Holy Spirit to help you live your life truly surrendered to God, no matter the cost. God convicts to deliver us while the devil condemns to destroy us. You must know the difference. Faith and obedience go hand-in-hand. Father God is not obligated to your dreams. He is committed to His holy purpose in you.

Jeff and I have come to realize that if we are not in the Word, it is really hard for us to tell the difference between the truth and lies. The enemy will always try to punk you in your mind. He will try to keep you from spending time with Father God. When you stop enjoying God, you stop growing and glowing. In His presence is fullness of joy. Remember, it is a choice to spend time with Him. The same men in the Bible who couldn't pray for one hour were able to fish all night (Luke 5:5). Priorities always matter. Is holy living a priority?

We all stumble when we put our faith in people, but faith in God keeps us from faltering. Have you tried and failed to live out holiness in your own strength? The Lord doesn't want you to settle for a life of just existing. He wants you to have a holy, happy life. So, don't accept anything less than a passionate relationship with your Father God and your spouse, if you are married. Actually, all great relationships are full of passion! Let Him help you and stretch you. You will not break. Breakthrough is coming! He is making room for His promises. He is making room for His holy impact through your life.

On this journey of becoming healed and holy in your relationships, however, you may discover that healing can be offensive to those people who benefit from your brokenness. These people aren't loyal to you; they are loyal to their need for you. Once their needs change so does their loyalty. Allow the Holy Spirit to heal you without becoming like those who hurt you. Remind yourself "...the one who is in you is greater than the one who is in the world" (1 John 4:4). Remember, despite what others are doing or saying around you, God is at work in you. When things are rough and you find yourself flat on your back, so to speak, and unable to move forward, the only way to look is up, so keep your focus on your holy Father God. What should have taken you out was a setup, not a setback, for the greatest comeback ever! You will only become stronger, wiser, and more anointed as you keep your focus on Jesus and His love and purpose for you instead of other people and your current circumstances.

We must live and be consumed with God's eternal purpose for our lives. This won't get rid of problems, but it will give you the power to overcome them. His purpose is eternal, and when we are in His presence our perspective changes. We see from the position of victory. Do not allow the enemy to win what he has already lost.

Satan only wins if we believe his lies. A lie will keep you living in shame from your past when God wants you to live in freedom for a better future. The enemy will always exaggerate your failures and inadequacies. He sows suspicion, jealousy, self-pity, and offers empty promises. The seed of life can only produce life, and the seed of death can only produce death. Seeds will always produce their own kind. We have to check the fruit that we are producing in our life to know what type of seeds we have planted. Keep your eyes on your Father God, and His truth and you will sow seeds of holiness.

Your spiritual enemy's strategy is to win the battle of your mind so that you will believe lies and live defeated. The root of all sin is unbelief in the Word of God. When you mistake lies for truth, it will hold you back from doing what God has purposed for you to do. Faith-people expect to win; fear-people expect to be defeated.

To help guard against defeat, seek out a "faith family" to support you and cheer you on (more about faith families in a chapter to follow). Ask these power-prayer partners to get in agreement with God's Word over your life and your relationships and help you go to the next level. Jeff and I have been so blessed with a faith family made up of our natural family, pastors, church family as well as other brothers and sisters in Christ. This group has come alongside us and held our arms up in prayer over the years. These folks are the remnant that chose to fight for us as we fought for each other. It is so important that you understand that when you submit to God and you allow Him to break that yoke of bondage, the entire unholy system will go down! Ordinary becomes extraordinary through prayer that is in agreement with the Word of God. Ask your faith family to actively participate in that with you!

We must remember that God purposes, Jesus provides, and the Holy Spirit performs. Don't lose sight of your divine destiny to be holy. Keep at it. Don't quit living a holy life. Don't bailout. Don't move on. Don't draw back. Father God sees you, hears you, and knows you. Stay in the fight of faith, and stay in His Word. Don't bow down to culture, instead influence it with God's love. This means that when you act upon the fact that you are wired for love, you will shock people. You will forgive more than others think is safe. You won't get offended. You will give more than others think is practical. You will expect more than others think is possible. You will love even when you are not loved back. Holiness in action!

“

Whatever kind of “pit” you are in, there is a way out.

”

ROUND

14

Scars, Sin, and Storms

Everyone has scars from relationships. We all get hurt, but we don't need to be ashamed of our scars. Don't hide them! Instead, consider your scars as proof of God's mercy, grace, and faithfulness. If you have scars, you're still alive. You've survived! Power and authority are a product of those scars.

I can testify that everything changed when the scars of Jesus met the broken, wounded places in me. The shame game was over, and I entered the throne zone. It is then that I also realized that pain is the same for everyone. No one has a patent on pain. When we choose to apply faith, love, and perseverance to our pain those obstacles turn into opportunities.

Whatever your story is, it is still being written. Don't let anyone define you by your scars or a bad chapter. The script is not complete, so keep going. The enemy and others thought you would have quit by now, but endurance frustrates Satan and produces victory. Don't let temporary circumstances make you give up on your long-term investments. Move forward with yourself and in your relationships with endurance.

Though the circumstances in my marriage were heartbreaking and scar-inducing, I made a choice to invest in my marriage and work toward a positive future with my husband. One thing that helped me was learning to celebrate the little wins and see the miracle milestones. Also, even though there were so many things that I could not understand, I was comforted by that phrase in Proverbs 3:5 that tells us "lean not on your own understanding." The Bible is warning us that our own understanding is lacking and dangerous. Our heart is deceitful, our emotions are fickle, and only God knows and understands all. I knew I would open the door to regret in my life if I made permanent decisions based on temporary emotions and my own understanding.

I set up some healthy boundaries for myself. For instance, I wouldn't let myself be an investigator. It was tempting to want to bombard Jeff with questions each time I learned he slipped up, so I could know the details of his affairs. It was also tempting to want to sneak around to try to catch him doing something wrong, but I quickly learned that doing these things was more hurtful than helpful. I had to trust that God would expose the truth that I needed to know. This made me a better responder and less of a reactor.

In addition to the boundaries I made for myself, I also made the decision to stay in love. I understood my inability to change my husband and others around me, but I did have the ability to influence. I also knew that emotions accompanied all my thoughts, and I needed to think like Jesus. What was Jesus like? Jesus ate with sinners. Jesus did not sin with them. I had to know the difference. I also knew that compassion without conviction is chaos. God won't endorse sin no matter how much He loves you. We can't get Him to do something for us that goes against His character and His Word, so don't bother asking Him to sanction your sin or the sin of others. He won't because He is holy. Through my pain and in my scars, God was (and is) true to Himself: merciful, gracious, compassionate, full of understanding…holy. I wanted to think and respond to Jeff in Jesus-ways because I knew that was truly the only way to really live.

Our Father God is also our provider. He always provides a way out for us when we are caught in the snare of sin. There are many forms of "pits" in our lives (self-pity, anger, resentment, and selfishness to name a few). Pits are even worse than ruts. The problem is not the pit but staying in it. We are responsible for seeking a way out. We may find ourselves thrown into a pit or we may jump into one by our own accord. Are you in a pit that has formed because of a choice you made or by how you reacted to the actions of someone else? If so, regardless of how you ended up in it, don't let the pit get into you. This is what makes you "pitiful." You can not make the pit your home. Don't believe the lie that you are supposed to live in the pit. We were never created to live in dark places. Bask in the truth of John 8:12, "Jesus spoke again to the people, he said, 'I am the light of the world. Whoever follows Me will never walk in darkness, but will have the light of life'."

We have all experienced the consequences of our choices, both good and bad. The good news is "...that in all things God works for the good of those who love him, who have been called according to his purpose" (Romans 8:28). We don't have the ability to solve our own problems, but God can, will, and already has! It is important to acknowledge the pit you may be facing or are already in, but always remember there are faithful promises you can claim that will get you out and over.

I have even more great news! God makes choices too, and forgiveness is His favorite one! He forgives so quickly and so often that the Word says it's His habit. "If you, GOD, kept records on wrongdoings, who would stand a chance? As it turns out, forgiveness is your habit, and that's why you're worshiped" (Psalms 130:3-4, MSG).

As I navigated my marriage and my husband's sin, it was imperative for me to begin admitting my own imperfections while realizing they did not make me a failure. The truth is, in all relationships both people have faults. One may have more faults than the other, but neither one is perfect. We have all fallen short. All of our relationships are a mixed-up bag of good and bad. We help lay a foundation for healing and love when we admit our own failures. This doesn't mean we accept full responsibility for the issues in a relationship, but we're also not blaming the other person for our own actions. The Bible says that love covers a multitude of sins. We also love by having a right view of our own sin.

It should take the pressure off when you know that God's grace is enough. We serve the God of the comeback! We don't serve a God who loses. In the Bible, Samson lost his power because he abandoned his purity. Samson left his principles. Maybe you have abandoned your purity and principles. If so, don't be deceived and believe that if you leave the things of God you won't lose. It is time to come back so you can get back. If you leave spending time with God, you lose relationship. If you leave prayer, you lose His presence (not because He has left you). There is power in the comeback. If you want to get back what you've lost, you must go back to the King! No one can make a success out of sin. If you want a blessed marriage, go back to your first love–Jesus. If you want blessed relationships, churches, businesses, health, and anointing, you must go back to your first love–Jesus. You must do the things you did first. Break the curse of compromise. The great news is when you come back you can get it back. No matter your sin or circumstance, choose the comeback with Jesus.

We are to be influencers and culture changers. Don't let shame continue to write your story! Don't let pit stops paralyze you on your way to the palace. Don't become comfortable in the pit! Let me encourage you again to read the story of Joseph. Take note of his attitude and how it adjusts in light of God's promise. Remember you are not alone. Ask the Holy Spirit for wisdom to get out of any pit you are in. Then, make a move!

Besides the pits of life that we encounter either by our own sin or the sin of others, there are also, as we all know, storms in life. Some are secret storms. Secret storms come out in our words or actions, but they form when we believe the lie Satan loves to tell us that if God was really with us, there would be no storm. If God was really with us, life would be smooth sailing. When we believe that lie, we blame others, ourselves, and even God for whatever storm we are going through. We think we should not have family problems, financial issues, broken relationships, work struggles, the loss of loved ones, etc., and we wonder why we can't see God in those moments. Physical vision is impaired in a storm, so you must look through faith eyes (eternal vision) instead. We must choose to walk by faith and not by sight. God does His best work in our lives when we are in trouble, broken, and distraught. No matter the storm you are in, He is in the middle of it with you. He is a very present help in times of trouble! He promises to be with you and never leave nor forsake you. I have to continuously remind myself of His many promises. The enemy does all he can to make us doubt God's promises, but don't fall for it. When God promises you something you may not have it in the physical realm, but it is a promise to come. Also, He promises when you pass through the water He will be with you. You are not swimming alone. Ever. He's with you in your current storm and in the storms to come.

“Real love doesn’t have a personal agenda.”

ROUND 15

Come Home, Have a Comeback

Do you know the story in the Bible about the prodigal son? If you don't know it or haven't read it in a while, I encourage you to check out Luke 15:11-32. Here is a brief summary: A son asks his father to give him his inheritance early. He then leaves his father's house and sets out on his own, making the choice to live a reckless and indulgent life. After squandering all of his money, the son finds himself destitute and starving. Miserable and broken, he decides to humble himself and go back to his father. His plan is to admit that he is no longer worthy to be called his son and ask his father if he would bring him on as one of his servants. While the son is heading home, his father sees him coming a long way off and runs out to meet him. Before the son even has a chance to speak, his father throws his arms around him and kisses his boy. He is filled with compassion for him! He then throws a party in his honor to celebrate that his prodigal son has come home.

Have you acted like a prodigal in some way? If you've left your Father God's presence, you probably never imagined the damage in your life that decision could cause you. When the prodigal in the story first left his father, he never thought he would lose. In the beginning, the son thought he was winning. He was having a good 'ole time! But none of us can leave the Father's house and win. To take this a step further, we also can't leave relationships and win. We may think things will be better if we take off, but the winning is found in the staying and in the loving. Of course, I'm not talking about staying in a relationship where you are being abused and are in danger. If we leave, we lose when we stay gone. The good news, however, is that your Father God is waiting for your comeback! He's waiting to welcome you home. "...His compassions never fail" (Lamentations 3:22).

When it comes to your relationship with Father God, examine what you have turned away from. You can't leave worship, prayer, and seeking His presence and think you won't lose. You can't leave the farm and harvest the crops. You can pick your choices, but you can't pick your consequences. Sin has consequences. It is time to own up and come home. Samson, when he realized he had lost due to his choices, humbled himself and asked the Lord to return his strength. The Lord did as Samson requested, and his comeback was his greatest moment. It is time to have comebacks in every area of your life.

To have a comeback, you have to confront a few

things. For instance, stop lying to yourself. When we stop lying to ourselves, we stop lying to everyone else. Confront this character issue, and you will have more confidence. You won't have to spend your energy trying to cover up your lies! Confront your chaos, and stop the cycle of dysfunction. This means taking action and taking responsibility. The greatest trouble in most of our lives is when we become passive or disengaged from the things of God. Of course, there are times when the challenges of responsibility will make you want to walk away from those you love. But I know from experience, we have to choose to be engaged. Choose to come home.

Most of the time, if we have lost passion in our relationships it's because we moved from our positions. Choose to stay in a position of love. Choose to stay in Christ. I'm not sure where I initially heard this (or a version of it), but I think it highlights what it means to stay in an active position of love and commitment to others:

- Don't just go to church, be in church.
- Don't just have children, be a parent.
- Don't just have parents, be a son or daughter.
- Don't just have a job, be a partner.
- Don't just have a spouse, be a helpmate.

When it comes to family relationships, just because you show up at home, it doesn't mean you are fulfilling your position there. It is time to stop just standing around. Yes, we have all made mistakes, been hurt, felt uncertain, have a past, and have stumbled and fallen, but today take your position of praise and purpose and tell the enemy and everyone around you, "I am here to stay! I will not be a victim and blame others anymore. I will be victorious! I am taking my place. I am getting off the fence (offense) and getting back into my rightful spot!" Your true partners and purpose will be birthed when you take your position and stay planted even through storms and droughts! You will never be perfect, but you'll be planted, present, and positioned! Planting is a covenant move. The place of power is when we stop running from ourselves and others. We don't need new places, we need a new attitude–the attitude of Jesus. The attitude of love never fails.

“Forgiveness is freedom.”

Faith Family

I talked a bit in Chapter 13 about seeking out a faith family to give you support and cheer you on in life. These folks can help guard you against defeat, and you can be that treasured faith family member for someone else. So, let's look at what it means to have a real friendship, be a real friend, and not take things personally in order to advance the Kingdom together.

Did you know that the deepest need of the human heart is for intimacy? That's just another way of saying friendship. Now, I'm not talking about casual acquaintances or fake friends but true faith friends. Of course, God is our ultimate comforter and best friend. The Lord hears our every prayer, collects all of our tears, and has already taken care of any doubt we may have. But He provides us with friendships (a faith family) here on earth, and they are a gift. Have the courage to not only step into life with these people for your sake but also for theirs. Watch and you'll see God do things in your relationships that only He can do! It's a blessing to have a faith family and a privilege to be this kind of friend to others.

Consider some of these characteristics of a true friend and examine the roles you play in the lives of others and the roles they play in your life:

A true friend sharpens.

They will make you a sharper, better person. Proverbs 27:17 says, "As iron sharpens iron, so one person sharpens another."

A true friendship will put an edge on your life.

False friends dull your life, blunt your influence, and drag you down. They don't speak the Word over you. Anybody who makes it easier for you to do wrong is not a true friend. One of the true tests of any friendship is asking yourself, "Am I a better person for having known this person?" and "Do they bring out Jesus in me?"

A true friend stays close. A true friend is steadfast.

"A friend loves at all times, and a brother is born for a time of adversity" (Proverbs 17:17). If you want to see who your real friends are, just make a mistake and see whether or not they leave you. I have learned that life is like a ship. Some people get on and off-board very easily. Some will stay on board as long as everything is sailing smoothly, but let the rough weather come, and they will abandon the ship.

A true friend is the one who will stick with you. A true friend's love stabs you.

You say, "But I don't want to be stabbed!" Proverbs 27:6 says, "Wounds of a friend can be trusted, but an enemy multiplies kisses." I like how the NASB version puts it: "Faithful are the wounds of a friend, but deceitful are the kisses of an enemy." A friend who really loves you will wound you if it's necessary. That is, they will tell you the truth and won't give you hypocritical kisses when they need to do a little spiritual surgery on you. Flattery is not true friendship.

A true friend cares enough to confront you but always remains in love.

I'm so grateful that throughout my life I've had those who would put their arms around my shoulders and help me when I've done wrong.

This caliber of friendships doesn't just happen. We don't make them overnight. They require investment, and they take time. Friendships are not toadstools; they are oak trees. Jesus said, "...Love each other as I have loved you" (John 15:12). Love is to be nurtured. Do you want to be a true friend? Then be accepting of others. We all want people to accept us. Jesus accepted the disciples. He said, "You did not choose me, but I chose you…" (John 15:16). Jesus did not accept the disciples because they were perfect but because they needed Him.

To be a good friend, you have to give recognition to others. I had to learn to give people my full heart and attention. This was something I failed at for years because of my own brokenness. I had to learn that when I talked with people it was important to also listen to them. Actually, it's more important to listen than to speak! When we listen, we're saying, "You're important to me. I acknowledge your presence and your worth." This is of utmost importance with our own families and with those we spend regular time with. It's so easy to take each other for granted and open the door for the enemy to come in and bring offense. It's also crucial to appreciate others. Tell your husband, your wife, your children, or your friends what you appreciate about them.

True friendship is costly. It's not easy to maintain a friendship/faith family. Remember John 15:13? "Greater love has no one than this: to lay down one's life for one's friends." That's a tall order! Yes, a friend loves at all times, but that is easy when times are good, yet what about when times are bad? Ask God to help you be a good friend, regardless.

If you are married, your most significant friendship is the one you share with your spouse. This relationship can't thrive or even survive without dedication, maintenance, and effort. I knew that if I was willing to put effort into rescuing my marriage, miracles could and would happen. To thrive, a healthy marriage relationship (and any relationship) requires humility. Recognize any hurtful way in yourself. Stopping and breaking the cycle of a broken relationship dynamic requires a change in your mindset. Not just one small change but radical God-changes. Taking responsibility for you and your part is a great starting point. One person's ability to do this can change the chemistry of the relationship! This means it doesn't take two to make a thing go right, though two will make it go better and faster. Studies have proven that most couples have issues because one or both partners shut down, withdraw, and isolate due to feelings of hurt, anger, and resentment. These are signs of a marriage (our most significant friendship) in deep trouble.

As you lean into each other, listen, have compassion, show empathy, operate in mercy, and don't lean back. It is scientifically proven (look up Dr. Gottman's study) that it takes five positive interactions to neutralize a negative interaction we've had with our partner. Be committed to participating and even initiating positive interactions, especially after a negative one. This isn't easy, of course, but it's effective. The secret weapon for couples and all relationships is don't give up! Here are some tools to help you lean in:

- Shut your mouth, but still, lean in! That means if you can't say something nice don't say anything at all. Don't be critical and blame. Express yourself, but do it in love. When there is a conflict or issue, choose to fight for the rebound. Don't avoid conflict, just choose to come back and handle your spouse, friend, or family member with care.

- Keep your divine vision in front of you. Look through the eyes of your heart. You must stay focused on the big picture and not the minor details. Remember, anger is usually just a symptom of fear, hurt, and frustration. Ask questions and talk heart-to-heart and not hurt-to-hurt. As you begin to communicate heart-to-heart, you are building a safe place in your relationship. This is a game-changer for all relationships!

- Choose to be a friend. Think about the positive points in your relationship. Even if you are struggling with the other person's flaws, express words of hope by regularly encouraging them. Point out one encouraging thing to them every day! Look for common ground and ways to stay in agreement. Don't shut yourself off from communication and spend time regularly investing in your relationships. Speak the truth in love.

How easy it is to fall back into the blame game when hurt, anger, and resentment set into any relationship. We either blame our partner, blame others, and/or blame ourselves. This is part of the cycle of dysfunction. We no longer address the issue at hand and instead enter into a vicious cycle of resentment, frustration, and anger. When this happens, we need to go back to not taking things personally. Remember Ephesians 6:12: "For our struggle is not against flesh and blood, but against the rulers, against the authorities, against the powers of this dark world and against the spiritual forces of evil in the heavenly realms." Of course, Satan doesn't want us to have vibrant, healthy relationships and enjoy a dedicated faith family! So, he does what he can to throw them into chaos.

Don't give up on relationships. Choose to lean into Jesus, then each other. While it's easy to want to give up when your friend or partner retreats, reacting increases the divide between you. Decide to take responsibility for warming things up, and begin to walk in love. Speak life. Speak hope. Speak truth. (Truth is what the Word of God says about you and others and this must be your reference source and final word.) Speak the Word of God over you and your spouse or friend. There's great power in the truth and this is all a part of being a member of a faith family.

It is so important to be honest about your thoughts, feelings, and dreams. If we are not honest then we become resentful. If your relationships are not safe places for these types of conversations, tell God about it. I try to always talk to God first about everything, and then let the Holy Spirit lead me when to talk to others. (Sometimes I have done this well, but other times I have gotten in the way and set off atomic emotional bombs.) Also, ask yourself: "Am I listening well to my friend, spouse, or family member?" One of the first defenses against anger is listening! And don't just listen in order to reply, but listen to hear their heart. "Understand this, my beloved brothers and sisters. Let everyone be quick to hear [be a careful, thoughtful listener], slow to speak [a speaker of carefully chosen words and], slow to anger [patient, reflective, forgiving];" (James 1:19, AMP).

Also, here's something radical: Go ahead and forgive first. Forgiveness does not mean you agree with the hurtful actions, but it will allow you to build a bridge over them and move on. Remember you are on the same team. Realize people do the best they can, and we all need forgiveness. Trust God over all your emotions and opinions. There's probably something about the situation/conflict that you do not understand, but God knows it all, and you can trust Him. If you haven't already, do yourself a favor and commit Proverb 3:5 to memory. "Trust in the LORD with all your heart and lean not on your own understanding;" (Proverbs 3:5). We all break promises as humans–promises to ourselves and to others–but Father God is the promise keeper. He is trustworthy.

Let faith work through love–God's love. Believe that Father God has you and your relationships in the palm of His hand. The work He began in you will be a good, completed work! So do your part to be a real friend to your faith family, your spouse, and others as you trust in Him.

"I believe in being a thermostat and not a thermometer"

ROUND

17

Laugh It Up!

When was the last time you had a sweet time sharing a laugh with someone? Our relationships need the element of laughter. The Bible says there is "...a time to weep and a time to laugh" (Ecclesiastes 3:4). When was the last time you allowed yourself to laugh or were able to laugh even when things were less than perfect in your life and in your relationships?

"Sarah said, 'God has brought me laughter, and everyone who hears about this will laugh with me'" (Genesis 21:6). The story of Sarah, Abraham, and Isaac is something most of us have heard or read. God promised to give Abraham and Sarah a son, but because of their old age it was not only miraculous, it was also comical. I personally believe God has a sense of humor, and one evidence of this is that Sarah became pregnant and gave birth to Isaac when she was 90-years-old! In fact, the name Isaac means "he laughs" in Hebrew. Sarah knew that not only would she laugh but others would laugh with joy along with her. In your life today, something may seem impossible in the physical, but I encourage you to go ahead and laugh at your future knowing Father God has you. He's with you in your struggles and "impossibilities."

"Consider it pure joy, my brothers and sisters, whenever you face trials of many kinds, because you know that the testing of your faith produces perseverance. Let perseverance finish its work so that you may be mature and complete, not lacking anything"

(James 1:2-4). This verse is a promise! Any challenges you may be dealing with in your relationships have a purpose. The Bible tells us to consider our challenges with joy. Ask the Father today to help you see the joy in every situation.

Proverbs 17:22 in The Message says this: "A cheerful disposition is good for your health; gloom and doom leave you bone-tired." The King James Version says, "A merry heart does good like medicine..." One definition of the adjective merry is, "festive and full of fun and laughter." This scripture reminds us that laughter is medicine. It has been proven that your body needs laughter. We know that during a laugh the human body begins to transform. Your blood pressure goes down, your immune system is built up, calories are burned, and this is just the beginning! Go ahead and laugh it up! Nehemiah 8:10 says, "...the joy of the Lord is your strength." Laughter has the power to change your vitality! The physical act of laughing releases endorphins in the brain, causing a sense of happiness. Some people say laughter is addictive, and this is one addiction you don't need to stop. God supports this addiction! Laughing increases your body's production of antibodies and T-cells that fight off disease and boost your immune system. Laughing together with others makes us feel relaxed, safe, comfortable, and less anxious and worried.

Our Father God gave us all the amazing ability to laugh. It was His idea, His design. The Word of God even tells us that God laughs. Because He is holy, He laughs at what the wicked think they can accomplish. "The wicked plot against the righteous and gnash their teeth at them; but the Lord laughs at the wicked for he knows their day is coming" (Psalm 37:12-13).

I was never given a middle name, but when I was around three years old, I began to tell everyone that my name was Allison Joy. Why? Because I knew even then that the joy of the Lord was my strength. This fruit of joy has been medicine to my broken heart, tired body, and worried mind many times since. Knowing that real joy (a fruit of the Spirit, see Galatians 5:22-23) lives on the inside of me has given me much strength in times when I've felt like I didn't have any.

This joy is not just mine but anyone who believes in Jesus! If you are a believer, then you are in Christ and learning to be Christ-like. You have joy at your disposal. This joy is contagious! It's a blessing to those you interact with. Jeff and I have chosen to laugh together, and that has not been a frivolous choice. It has been effective medicine in our relationship, and laughter is a by-product of righteous living. Proverbs 31:25 says that a virtuous woman "...can laugh at the days to come." This also means that we can laugh at the enemy. When the enemy has taken advantage of us, we're not left high and dry. We simply get the Jesus-advantage. Jesus went through hell and prospered. We can take advantage of everything the enemy does and prosper in the process as God does His work, which is greater than anything Satan can do! So let joy be your strength. Exercise your joy and choose to laugh today!

“Do not allow the enemy to win what he has already lost.”

ROUND

18

Liar, Liar, Pants On Fire

The Truth sets you free. So you may be asking yourself, "How can I live free from the lies I tell myself, the lies others tell me, and the lies the enemy tells me?" The only way to live free is to live in Jesus. He is where truth is found. He is Truth! And, He wants you to be truthful.

In John 4:1-42 you'll find the famous story about the woman at the well. As Jesus is having a conversation with this woman, He tells her to go get her husband and come back to the well. She tells Him she has no husband and He replies, "You are right when you say you have no husband. The fact is, you have had five husbands, and the man you now have is not your husband. What you have just said is quite true." When we answer Him truthfully, freedom rushes in. This woman is changed. Her eyes are opened to the truth of who Jesus is. He then says in that same passage, "God is spirit, and his worshipers must worship in the Spirit and in truth." This means truth is reality. We must be real, be honest, and tell the truth to honor God and to be free!

Truth is defined as "the true or actual state of a matter." As we learn in John 17:17, "...God's word is truth," so we can use God's Word to be set free from the lies we've allowed ourselves to believe. We have to speak the truth over ourselves and our situations and to the people in our lives. We have to replace the lies with God's truth, and we do that when we get the Word on it! Here is the truth: The person to your left is a liar. The person to your right is a liar. The person sitting in your very seat is a liar. We're all liars, but we can become truth-seekers, speakers, and builders by living a Spirit-led life and filtering everything through the Word of God.

Do you know how to stop deception in your life and in relationships? You have difficult conversations with difficult people even during difficult times. We have to stop lying to ourselves first before we can stop lying to everyone else! Deception is not a game; it is serious business. It is the tool the enemy uses to kill, steal, and destroy.

The Bible tells us in Titus 1:2 that God doesn't lie. God is Truth. It's not possible for Him to lie because it's not in His nature. Father God wants His creation to be marked by truth, too. Relationships are built on trust, and trust is built on truth. If you don't have truth, you won't have trust. If you don't have trust, you will never have true fellowship. God knew what He was doing when He set up the plan for being honest. He wants us to be guided by truth, so we can reflect Him. Honesty has always been the best policy! Since the beginning, He has always desired for His people to be truth-bearing and truth-telling.

We're told in Ephesians 4:25, "Therefore each of you must put off falsehood and speak truthfully to your neighbor, for we are all members of one body." Paul is saying that truth is part of our identity in Christ. The Church in Ephesus was instructed to see their lying ("falsehood") as a part of their old self that died when they invited Christ into their life. Lying was like old, dirty-smelling, sweaty clothes that they had cast off, and Paul was encouraging them not to put those back on. He told them they were new creations in Jesus, and they needed to put on the new clothes–the clothes of truth-telling. This was a new wardrobe that was given in Christ by the power of His Spirit. Truth was essential to them and their relationships just like it is to us for our fellowship with each other. It's just one of the ways we honor God's name. We, as Christ-followers, need to be a part of creating a community that is built on trust and truth. Lying will always fracture any foundation. It is time we repented against untruth and renewed our minds by what God's Word says about our truthful God and His commands for us to walk in truth. We also have to seek to rebuild the relationships we have with brothers and sisters in Christ who have been broken by the sin of lying, of falsehood. Do not let the struggle of false testimony define you and destroy your relationships. Jesus has made the way for truthful living. We must cling to His Word, commit to truth, and know that we are able to be promise-keepers and truth-speakers when we follow Him!

"...but endurance
frustrates Satan
and
produces victory."

ROUND 19

Seeing Your Marriage as God Does

These last few chapters will focus almost solely on the relationship of marriage, however, many of the concepts and truths highlighted–like, loyalty and making the choice to love–translate to other relationships as well. So, whether or not you are married, I encourage you to read on!

Marriage was part of God's perfect plan from the beginning. God established it before the fall, while man was still sinless. We read in Genesis 2:18 (AMP) that Father God said, "Now the Lord God said, 'It is not good (beneficial) for the man to be alone; I will make him a helper [one who balances him—a counterpart who is] suitable and complementary for him'." When man had no pressures and would be considered perfect, he was still incomplete without a helpmate. Father God saw Adam's need without Adam even asking for it. Adam was unaware of what he was missing, but God initiated the marriage because that was His perfect plan. This means that Father God holds marriage in a high position. Do you hold marriage in a high position?

Sadly, many people, even believers, put very little effort into their marriage. Because of this, they have received very little out of marriage. Many couples have no idea of what God intends marriage to be, so they settle for what they see around them. They make the excuse that everyone has marital issues, so it's just the way it is. We think conflict is a normal part of marriage, so we settle for it (instead of addressing it in the right way), or we just leave the relationship. According to World Population Review, as of 2021, almost 50% of married couples in the U.S. divorce, but trouble in marriage doesn't have to be our reality. Father God has made it possible for us to enjoy a healthy marriage. He created marriage, so He certainly knows how to make it function properly! Ephesians 5:22-33 has a lot to say about how we are to be towards one another in marriage, and it all points to love. God's kind of love. This kind of love makes a marriage a God-filled one.

We should know who and what we are in Christ and what we have because of Him. If we know these things, we will realize that we are kings and queens who sit in heavenly places with Christ. That will give us a good self-image! Many marriages are faltering because two people who don't love themselves are trying to love each other. But when you think about it, they can't really love their mate when they don't love themselves.

Couples cannot operate toward each other with

carnal love and expect a solid marriage. Carnal love is motivated by emotions or senses, but God's love comes from the heart. Although the feelings are definitely affected, they should not be the driving force. God's love is the same yesterday, today, and forever. A spouse who loves when they're in the mood but acts the opposite when their mood changes is operating in carnal "love," not in God's love. God's love makes a different choice. You may feel like being angry, but you can choose to operate in love when you're operating in God's love. You can choose and act on love even when you don't feel like it. Matthew 5:44 tells us to even love our enemies (and sometimes we can see our spouse as our enemy)! This is a command. Father God didn't say, "Love if you feel like it."

Choosing and acting on God's love and not carnal love is a process, and I want to encourage you to enjoy the process! Choose to do what God's Word tells you to in your marriage, and you'll be surprised at how your feelings will follow. You can train yourself to love with God's kind of love. Our feelings are corrupted. In Christ, we have His promise that our spirits have been totally changed. "Therefore, if anyone is in Christ, the new creation has come: The old has gone, the new is here" (2 Cor. 5:17). Galatians 5:22 says that love is a part of the Fruit of the Spirit. Our feelings are not automatically changed, but we can choose our attitudes and actions. Our feelings will change when we put them under the control of the Holy Spirit. It is an act of faith when we act on love! God's kind of love is a choice that you make on the basis of what God has said and then act on it in faith until it becomes a reality in your spirit, soul, and body.

God's love is never based upon what we do for Him or what we deserve but upon His choice to love us. Period. Father God chose to give it to us when He sacrificed His Son for our benefit, and He chooses to love us each day. God's love is unconditional. Jesus didn't wait until we were worth it or had repented before He gave Himself for our sins. He gave Himself for us while we were yet sinners (Romans 5:8). It is our choice to put this unconditional love of God to work in our marriages. In marriage, we see each other at our worst and are wise to give mercy, not justice. We have to choose to give the unconditional love of God. When we do, our relationship becomes a beautiful adventure.

A part of love is loyalty. Everyone has things or people to which he/she is loyal, like friends, sports teams, a favorite restaurant, the college you attended, etc. I grew up in a home where loyalty was lived out. As a result, I grew to love God and people. Love in action was demonstrated. For example, we always had an open-door policy. (I think that is what Father God's door is like!) I learned by example that the key was, no matter how good or bad things got, we were to stay loyal to the Word of God in how we love. It points out the treasure in everyone. Growing up in this environment taught me to be loyal even when the going gets tough, and believe me, it's hard to stay loyal to someone who is blowing it! It's just like when a team starts losing and you don't feel like cheering for them, but instead, you want to criticize every coach, player, official, and owner. This loyalty of love modeled for me, however, taught me to see the best in people and cheer for them rather than criticize, and I carried this mindset into my marriage. It helped me to be able to speak life to my husband and into our relationship when things got hard and it still does to this day. It has been said that the lack of loyalty is one of the major causes of failure in every walk of life. Jesus expresses to us a loyal love, one that said, "No matter what happens, I am here for you. I see the best in you. I gave myself up for you." This is the type of love that we have been invited to receive and told to give to our spouse (and others in our life). It's a love that never fails.

Jesus is the perfect example of our Father God's love. He loved and served His disciples as He washed their feet in the upper room (John 13). In this way, He gave them and us a tangible example of serving and loving others. In Romans 5:5 we're told that He supplies our love. "...God's love has been poured out into our hearts through the Holy Spirit, who has been given to us." He also teaches us to love. 1 Thessalonians 4:9 says, "...you yourselves have been taught by God to love each other." Now that is an amazing statement! We don't need a lecture on love; we are taught by God to do it. When we put into practice what we've learned, a remarkable love story is the result.

Today, the Father is teaching me more and more about His love, His truth, His loyalty. God shows us loyalty through relationships and His covenant. Throughout the Word, we see stories of loyalty. As followers of Christ, we show our loyalty by following His commands and each one is hinged on love. But even when we fail to be completely loyal, we have His promise that He will be loyal to us, and

He can help us remain loyal to our spouse. If you are struggling in this area, ask Him to help you choose loyal love.

How can we take inventory of our love journey in our marriage? One of the most important things is to check our words. Words are nuclear and they are eternal. They can hurt or heal, build up or destroy. They move God or the enemy. Also, do not allow anger to harden your heart toward your spouse. Whether you've been married for a long time or a short time or some time in between, choose forgiveness. Cut the invisible umbilical cord that feeds you from past hurts with God's scissors of unconditional love.

Hold your marriage in a high position, and you will be in agreement with God. Commit to speaking life into your marriage. The secret is letting the love of God work within you. Then, you will act in love because love is more interested in the other person than it is in itself, regardless of feelings. It doesn't take offense personally. When we begin operating in this realm of love–God's love and not carnal love–we will be blessed and we will bless our spouse and others.

> “Don’t let temporary circumstances make you give up on your long-term investments.”

ROUND

20

Careful With the Questions

When we are hurt by our spouse, friend, or family member we can be plagued by nagging curiosity. For example, each time I'd find out about one of Jeff's indiscretions, my mind would be filled with questions (among other things), and a part of me would want to demand answers. If you've ever found out that your spouse or someone close to you was disloyal, you probably have questions, too. This is normal, but I urge you to be careful with the questions. As I touched on in Chapter 14, I had to set a boundary for myself not to go there with my husband. Questions can be more hurtful than helpful.

It doesn't matter if you discover the lie or secret sin on your own, if someone else shares it with you, or if your spouse comes to you and confesses. I believe that however you find out, in addition to experiencing a jarring shock wave, hearing the truth can also bring with it a strange type of relief. But then, questions begin to form and they go around and around in your mind. The most common question that never has a good answer is, "Why?". Most questions that start with why don't need to be asked or answered. The truth is, for some questions–like a "why" question–the answer is never enough. This means that even if someone gives you an answer, it won't satisfy the pain in your heart nor truly answer the "why" in your mind. A time comes when it's wise to abandon the questions and move on. Move forward. By asking the Holy Spirit, you will know what questions to ask and when to stop asking certain questions. I began to ask myself, "Do I really need to know this answer?" "Will this help me heal or hurt me?" When you put your trust in God to make all things new again the questions will change. I only wanted to ask questions that would help us both heal and live free lives.

I also did not want to be offended every time we had a conversation. Maybe you have some relationships in your life (with a mother-in-law, a co-worker, a spouse, etc.) where you get offended during most conversations. I wanted to live out of forgiveness and unconditional love for Jeff. I wanted my life and marriage to be evidence of God's goodness and His love and power working through me and that couldn't happen if I was obsessed with getting all my questions answered. It's not all about us. I know that the more full of God we are, the less full of ourselves we will be. To grasp this, read Ephesians 3:14-19 (I recommend you read it more than once). "For this reason I kneel before the Father, from whom every family in heaven and on earth derives its name. I pray that out of his glorious riches he may strengthen you with power through his Spirit in your inner being, so that Christ may dwell in your hearts through faith. And I pray that you, being rooted and established in love, may have power, together with all the Lord's holy people, to grasp how wide and long and high and deep is the love of Christ, and to know this love that surpasses knowledge—that you may be filled to the measure of all the fullness of God."

I want to be filled with His fullness and not filled with curiosity over the details of how or why my husband was disloyal. Here is the truth: when we are hurt we are not in the greatest headspace. Normally we don't even have a biblical mindset while everything is crashing down. In times like this, I purposely open my Bible before I open my mouth. Every time I do that, God's Word cuts through all my justifications to stay hurt and angry. My case always crumbles when compared to Christ. Now, don't let the enemy condemn you for ways you've done it wrong in the past. (We've all done it wrong sometimes, by the way.) Today is the day you can do it the right way, God's way! The Holy Spirit will lead you on how to handle your situations; just keep your heart in a posture of love and forgiveness. Jesus even shows us through the Lord's prayer that forgiveness is to be a part of our everyday prayers. I am thankful that He loves and forgives first, showing us how we can do it through Him. Forgiveness may seem unfair in our culture ("That person doesn't deserve it!"), but the truth is, there is freedom in forgiveness.

Just like Adam and Eve, we don't run to forgiveness, we normally run from it. Forgiveness is not something that we can do on our own, but God does command us to assist in forgiveness. Are you willing? Demanding answers to your questions won't help you to forgive. It is also important to know that just because you walk in love and forgiveness, it doesn't mean that all relationships get restored. But God can redeem your life. To live this life of love takes Divine intervention, and that is exactly what God wants to give to you. Even as I am writing this and hard things continue in my life, love still never fails. Hard things will happen because we are humans in relationships. So, I will need to continually have heart-to-hearts with Jesus, keep my Bible open, and apply His Word to my life. It is important to remember that we can only heal what we are willing to deal with.

Many times over the years, I've had to put my hurts down on paper, give them to the Lord and then tear them up. God wants you to acknowledge the pain and take it to Him. Your story matters to Him. I've found that exercise to be more helpful than asking too many questions or asking the wrong questions to the person who has offended me. It is also important to have God-led boundaries. These boundaries should bring peace and freedom to your heart. When I see a guardrail along a bridge I never think, "I wish that wasn't there." No, my heart can rest knowing, if we had an accident, it is there to help protect us from death. Many times boundaries are there to stop us from going over the edge. We need boundaries on what we say, where we go, how we communicate, what questions we ask, etc. It is for safety and sanity that we set love boundaries. These boundaries will change over time, but boundaries make for healthier relationships. Remember we have to shut down all arguments, opinions, and excuses that go against the knowledge of God. So the Word of God has to be our first guardrail. "For though we walk in the flesh, we are not waging war according to the flesh. For the weapons of our warfare are not of the flesh but have divine power to destroy strongholds. We destroy arguments and every lofty opinion raised against the knowledge of God, and take every thought captive to obey Christ" (2 Corinthians 10:3-5 ESV).

No matter what we see or feel when an opinion or argument comes to our mind, if it goes against God's Word, we cannot entertain it. We don't want to be like Eve and change our eternal vision for an imperfect, carnal perspective. When you keep an eternal perspective, peace is the compass that will direct you, and the fear of the unknowns will be drowned out. Even though we live with the "flesh" sight of both good and evil, when we look through the eyes of our heart we see in the heavenly realm. We see through eyes of faith and not flesh. Maybe we don't see the final outcome, but we can trust our Father God's full perspective. When we stay tender toward the things of God we are in place for breakthrough and not breakdown. There is so much freedom when we live in peace. And a life of love and forgiveness produces peace. When you trade in all the drama for God's perspective, you will have peace. Jesus showed us and told us how to live.

In Matthew 6:9-15, Jesus even tells us how to pray. I especially like how The Passion Translation puts it. "Pray like this: 'Our Beloved Father, dwelling in the heavenly realms, may the glory of your name be the center on which our lives turn. Manifest your kingdom realm, and cause your every purpose to be fulfilled on earth, just as it is in heaven. We acknowledge you as our Provider of all we need each day. Forgive us the wrongs we have done as we ourselves release forgiveness to those who have wronged us. Rescue us every time we face tribulation and set us free from evil. For you are the King who rules with power and glory forever. Amen.' And when you pray, make sure you forgive the faults of others so that your Father in heaven will also forgive you. But if you withhold forgiveness from others, your Father withholds forgiveness from you." Forgiveness makes up almost half of the prayer! So, Jesus is saying not only do I want to take care of your needs, but I also want to take care of your heart. Just like eating, forgiveness is supposed to be part of our daily routine. I can tell you that for many years this was not part of my daily routine, but it is now more than ever. I don't want offenses to shape me.

Are you easily offended? Do you get defensive fast? Are you quick to get angry? I think that when the answer is "yes" to these questions we are normally slow to pray. Slow to forgive. Slow to have heart-to-hearts with heaven, and we end up in hurt-to-hurt conversations instead. It's a popular choice. In today's society, most people would rather take sides than take a knee for prayer. We all will feel offended, hurt, angry, used, resentful, and unloved at times. But feeling a certain way is different than living that way. We have to be quick to throw off our feelings and not feed the hurt by bombarding the person who hurt us with questions. Jesus did not just teach us how to pray for forgiveness, He showed us a lifestyle of forgiveness that was on the foundation of love. It is even what He said as His flesh was dying, "Father forgive them." That is what I've learned to say when my flesh is dying, too. It is a choice to let God's Word become the words of our story

"Don't let shame continue to write your story!"

ROUND

21

Better Together

We are better together. "A person standing alone can be attacked and defeated, but two can stand back-to-back and conquer. Three are even better, for a triple-braided cord is not easily broken" (Ecclesiastes 4:12 NLT). One person is an individual. Two people make a relationship. But, when we get to "three" we have community. Covenant community. We have become something we could never be on our own. Community (found in our faith family) is a strong cord! We have to be intentional to have healthy relationships. We have to forgive! We have to give mercy! We have to have unconditional love!

True connections take loyalty, commitment, and courage. Social media makes connection seem easy–just the click of a button. But our Father God calls us to deeper relationships. This means we must be intentional in all relationships–as a spouse, friend, parent, co-worker, sibling, child, etc. Our life seasons and circumstances impact our capacity for connection, but we can ask ourselves, "What can I do to truly connect with the people I love?" It is important to really see the people God has put in your life to love and connect with.

Being intertwined like a cord means choosing to stay in relationship, even when it's hard. We live in a fallen world, and we are fallen people. That means conflicts will inevitably come, personalities will clash, and disappointments will happen. But we become stronger when we learn to stay because the strands of a rope depend on each other. What happens to one strand, happens to all. We were created for community and to share life with one another through the good, the bad, and the ugly!

That's why I want every decision I make to be steeped in love. Relationships are covenants, not contracts, and that requires love. Relationships done right are a beautiful thing because, though we are different from each other, we are better together. God designed it that way, but it takes time to "come together." Understanding that marriage is a permanent promise–a covenant–has been a key to Jeff's and my endurance as a couple, especially when things are hard. Marriage brings with it a huge question. Will you spend the rest of your life with me? My answer to Jesus and to Jeff remains the same today as it did on our wedding day, "Yes, I will."

This decision has made me cry over the years, but it has also made me laugh. I have learned to see the absurdity in the squabbles. Who cares about how he squeezes the toothpaste or if she places the glasses upside down or right-side up in the cupboard? Don't take it personally or seriously. When we are a part of a relationship, we are wise to laugh about such things. Laughter brings lightness to the situation–I call them "laughter boosters." Also, try and find solutions even for these little offenses. Offer to buy your spouse their own tube of toothpaste, or squeeze it for him/her! And don't forget to kiss after you brush your teeth!

Stay focused on what really matters in your relationship and know that, even when it may feel like you and your partner are heading in different directions with the more serious issues, you have the same destination. I'm grateful that Jeff and I now know that where we are headed is good and we know we'll be together as Jesus is directing both of us. This means that we don't take highlight reels from our past and make them a reality over and over again. We go to the highlights in our Bibles and consult God's Word.

Over time, Jeff and I decided that the "D" word (divorce) was not allowed in our home to threaten each other. It could not be used as a tool to manipulate and control the other person. We chose to not permit it to be part of our language. Having this "rule" helped us to begin investing in each other instead of threatening each other. And when trouble would come and we could not find a compromise or solution, we would seek godly counsel. We learned to get help. This is one of the wisest decisions we ever made and we still make that decision today. We get help when we need it! We made a choice to seek the Lord together through prayer, Bible study, worship, iron-sharpening friends (faith family), and fasting, and it has made all the difference.

We also celebrate with each other. We've learned to cheer for each other instead of criticizing. This makes for a much better partnership. Even during times of frustration or difficulty, never let your heart be turned away from your partner. Remember, apart from your relationship with God, your marriage is the most important relationship in your life. The truth is your marriage is more important than your children, your job, your personal interests, and your hobbies. Choose to invest in meeting each other's needs, including celebrating each other, and refuse to sacrifice your marriage for emotions.

Base your marriage on Christ-like love (reread 1 Corinthians 13, "The Love Chapter" in several versions). Your marriage should be sacrificial and permanent. Marriage is a covenant designed by God. That means your marriage is based on the decision to love and cherish each other and not on feelings, convenience, or comfort. "For better or for worse, in sickness and in health, 'til death do us part" is certainly not based on feelings, convenience, or comfort! Make the effort to create and maintain a covenant marriage that can weather the storms of emotions, disagreements, and difficulties. Remember, marriage is God's design and if you're married, you are better together.

"Choose to come home."

ROUND

22

We Have To Fight For Love

As couples, when we encounter storms during our walk together, the key ingredient to getting on a smoother path is our attitude of love in action. We must have the absolute determination and resolve to stay in love! Marriage comes with bumps and sometimes mountains, and sometimes cliffs, and sometimes ocean views. Father God has given His love to us so it can flow through us. This means that we are equipped to handle the journey! And it is important to keep the fire of an everlasting flame of love lit. Marriage is not just a relationship of a man and a woman but also a three-way relationship that must include God. Actually, He must be the center of it all!

If you feel burned out, cold, or that the flame in your marriage has been reduced to a flicker, don't quit! Father God is smack dab in the center and He will help you. Let your marriage illuminate God's love! Let your life be a lighthouse of love. "So I give you now a new commandment: Love each other just as much as I have loved you. For when you demonstrate the same love I have for you by loving one another, everyone will know that you're my true followers" (John 13:34-35 TPT).

Looking back over the years of my marriage, it is shocking to me that I do not feel sad about our past. I do remember times when I actually thought I was drowning in my emotions. Over time, as I began to swim out of the deep, dark sea of my emotions, I found myself still getting caught in the waves and undertow of pain and fear. I continually cried out to the Lord for help, and in His faithfulness, He helped me to begin walking toward the shore. I would still get caught in the waves occasionally, but I wasn't drowning anymore. The miracle is that today I sit in my chair with my toes in the water and when I look out I see goodness and experience refreshment from my first love, Jesus. He was always with me, holding me, comforting me, protecting me, and loving me. For that reason, sadness is not a part of my story. Miraculous, isn't it?

I'm forever grateful that God has taught me that we don't win without love. If your marriage is a battle right now, don't go down to your partner's level and give the devil that satisfaction. Satan is trying to wreak havoc, but don't let him call the shots. You must fight the urge to get even with your spouse when you're hurt or angry. You can't win using the same weapons as your enemy (Satan is your real enemy, not your spouse), which include: anger, hate, unforgiveness, and judgment. Guard against contempt sneaking in. Contempt is aged anger that blinds you so that you can no longer see the good in someone. It makes you unable to remember any positive thing but causes you to only see and focus on the negative things. It kills the garden of your love! But God can make all things new with you and heal your hurts and melt your contempt. He breaks the spirit of offense and digs up the root of bitterness. One drop of the blood of Jesus can heal a lifetime of anger! But we must receive it by faith. Faith is the hand that takes the things we need from God. Everything Jesus purchased for us on Calvary can be obtained by faith, including salvation, healing, the fullness of the Spirit, the gifts of the Spirit, the fruit of the Spirit, and victory over the world, the flesh, the devil, and all the powers of darkness. As He hung naked on the cross, Jesus said, "...'Father, forgive them, for they do not know what they are doing'..." (Luke 22:34). He was saying to God, "Your promise is being fulfilled through me." Jesus and His ways are always the answer.

Because I know I can trust Him, I am committed to doing this marriage (and my other relationships) in God's way. I will not take offenses personally any longer. I will do His will, not my will. I'm all in and willing to fight for love. Sure, I will fail sometimes, but I will also experience victory in Jesus. How? This verse tells us: "My old identity has been co-crucified with Christ and no longer lives. And now the essence of this new life is no longer mine, for the Anointed One lives his life through me—we live in union as one! My new life is empowered by the faith of the Son of God who loves me so much that he gave himself for me, dispensing his life into mine!" (Galatians 2:20 TPT). Can I get an "amen?"

Friend, I so desperately, passionately want you to know that God has a plan, purpose, and promise for you. You are wanted. You are loved. What God has begun in you and in your relationships, He will finish. Just stay in the process. Stay humble. Stay surrendered. And don't take things personally. Remember,

God is love so stay in love through Him, and watch Him work out His master plan for your life.

Made in the USA
Coppell, TX
29 June 2022